HISTORIC PENNSYLVANIA

A Tour of the State's
Top 100 National Landmarks

Mindy Gulden Crawford

Globe
Pequot

Guilford, Connecticut

Globe
Pequot

An imprint of The Rowman & Littlefield Publishing Group, Inc.
4501 Forbes Blvd., Ste. 200
Lanham, MD 20706
www.rowman.com

Distributed by NATIONAL BOOK NETWORK

British Library Cataloguing in Publication Information available

Library of Congress Cataloging-in-Publication Data available

ISBN 978-1-4930-4185-5 (paperback)
ISBN 978-1-4930-4186-2 (e-book)

∞™ The paper used in this publication meets the minimum requirements of
American National Standard for Information Sciences—Permanence of Paper for
Printed Library Materials, ANSI/NISO Z39.48-1992

CONTENTS

SOUTHWEST

HISTORIC LANDMARKS: EXPLORING OUR PAST AND ADVOCATING FOR OUR FUTURE

The National Historic Landmark designation is an honor that requires a great deal of work on the part of the nominator and the National Park Service staff. Pennsylvania's inventory of National Historic Landmarks is impressive and tells a wonderful story about the founding of our nation and the state's fascinating history. Reviewing the list of 169 Pennsylvania National Historic Landmarks reveals a collection of some amazing places and interesting stories. Pennsylvania has so much history to be explored. While you can learn much from exploring the places included in this book, I hope you will also explore the ones that could not be included. Every listing is unique, intriguing, and surprising. But please don't stop there!

The stories of the special places contained in this book are important, each in their own way. If you mention to anyone that you are writing about 100 National Historic Landmarks, you are almost always asked which one is your favorite. There is no easy answer. My favorite is the one I am currently working on or the one I am about to work on. Immersing yourself into the history of a site is exciting and often surprising. For me the most unexpected discovery was how so many of these places are linked historically by the people responsible for their existence. Architects, builders, philanthropists, political leaders, innovators, and dreamers created these places and often were responsible for more than one of them, sometimes many. Learning the links between these stories helps to understand how connected we are to our past, present, and future. As I worked my way through each entry, I felt connected to George Washington and Ben Franklin and the other visionaries who created our nation. I am inspired by the engineering feats that resulted in the canal and railroad systems and brought water to our communities. I hope you will find yourself in their stories.

Do not think that if a site is not designated as a National Historic Landmark it is not historic or important. There are countless places in Pennsylvania that are historic and worthy of recognition and study. Just because they have not gone through the process of National Historic Landmark designation does not diminish their contribution to the story of Pennsylvania. There are almost 3,500 properties and districts listed on the National Register of Historic Places in Pennsylvania. Many of

the historic districts contain hundreds of individual properties. Pennsylvania is filled with historic places!

Any place that is important to you or your community that tells the history of your special place is also worthy of recognition. No one knows your story better than you. We are all responsible for caring for these places and letting others know why it is important to protect and preserve them. Become an advocate for your own history, in addition to the ones that are important to the state and to the nation.

Thompson Mayes, author of *Why Old Places Matter, How Historic Places Affect Our Identity and Well-Being* (Rowman and Littlefield, 2018) said, "The notion that old places matter is not primarily about the past. It is about why old places matter to people today and for the future. It is about why old places are critical to people's sense of who they are, to their capacity to find meaning in their lives, and to see a future." We are who we are today because of our past, and we must understand the role of our history for our future. A preservationist must face a hard truth—we can't save everything. Sometimes we lose places that are important and sometimes we save places that we thought would be impossible. Many historic places have found new uses and futures, not just as museums but as restaurants, schools, offices, and apartments. By recognizing the value of these places, we become defenders of them and their place in the future.

I have worked in the field of history and historic preservation for almost 40 years. Every day I learn something new that gets me excited to find out more. I hope this book will do that for you. Plan a road trip to see some of these places for yourself. Visit other places along the way and find new ones. Never stop exploring, and do not forget to take photographs!

Exterior of the Gifford
Pinchot House, see
entry on p. 2

Asa Packer Mansion
Packer Hill Ave., Jim Thorpe; (570) 325-3229; asapackermansion .com; open year-round; admission charged

The 1852 Asa Packer Mansion overlooks the town of Jim Thorpe (formerly Mauch Chunk) and is a remarkable high-style Italianate villa. Little has changed since the time of its construction. The mansion is three stories high with a two-story veranda, and the low-pitched roof is topped by an octagonal cupola. The mansion contains 17 rooms with elaborately carved woodwork. During the summer the mansion was "air-conditioned" with cool air from the nearby ice house. The installation of electricity in 1911 has been the only major change. The interior exists essentially as it did when the Packer family resided here from 1861 to 1912 with original furnishings, chandeliers, draperies, wallpaper, and carpets.

Asa Packer was born in Connecticut, leaving home at age 17 to apprentice as a carpenter with his cousin. He and his wife settled on a farm along the Susquehanna River in Pennsylvania. He spent winters using his carpentry skills to build and repair canal boats. In 1832 he traveled to Mauch Chunk, answering a call for men to captain coal barges on the Lehigh Canal. The Packer family settled there in 1833.

Packer knew that a faster system was needed, and he tried to convince the Lehigh Coal & Navigation Company to begin using a steam railway to transport anthracite coal. He was not successful. Then in 1851 he managed to take controlling interest of the Delaware, Lehigh, Schuylkill & Susquehanna Railroad Company (later the Lehigh Valley Railroad). Between 1852 and 1855 a railway line was built connecting Mauch Chunk to Easton and Allentown. The line eventually connected to Buffalo, New York, and New York City, and was used to transport anthracite coal.

There is some speculation that Packer's background in carpentry had some influence on the design of his home, but it was designed by architect Samuel Sloan of Philadelphia. The house bears a strong resemblance to a design published by Sloan in his 1852 *Model Architect.* Packer was a philanthropist throughout his life, giving thirty-three million dollars to the town of

Mauch Chunk and the Lehigh Valley and founding Lehigh University in Bethlehem. He was also active in politics, serving in the Pennsylvania House of Representatives and two terms in the US House of Representatives. At the time of his passing in 1879, he left an estate valued at $54.5 million.

His daughter, Mary Packer Cummings, lived in the home until her death in 1912. The home still contains one of her prize possessions, a 1905 Orchestrion, a Swiss-made music maker with organ, bells, and a drum. Mary left the family home and all its contents to the Borough of Mauch Chunk as a memorial to her father. In 1954 the Jim Thorpe Lions Club approached the Borough about opening the mansion's doors. In 1956 the mansion opened to visitors, and, in 1985, it was designated a National Historic Landmark.

Gifford Pinchot House (Grey Towers)
122 Old Owego Tpke., Milford; (570) 296-9630; greytowers.org; grounds open year-round with no admission charged; mansion tours available Thurs through Mon, Memorial Day through Oct; admission charged

Built from 1884 to 1886, this large stone mansion designed by architect Richard Morris Hunt was the home of Gifford Pinchot, first chief of the US Forest Service and Pennsylvania governor for two terms. James Pinchot was a wealthy wallpaper merchant, civic-minded, and a supporter of the arts. Hunt, an influential architect of the time, was a personal friend of James and Mary Pinchot, who made a point of socializing with many wealthy and prominent individuals. Hunt designed their summer home with 44 rooms and 23 fireplaces, utilizing both local materials and reflecting the French heritage of the Pinchot family. For two decades the Pinchots and their children enjoyed numerous summers at Grey Towers, entertaining guests for afternoon teas and dinner parties. James became increasingly concerned about the widespread logging of the area with no provisions made for the replanting of trees for the future. It was James who urged his eldest son, Gifford, to pursue a forestry career.

Gifford's most important contribution was his role as a conservationist and forester. He created the US Forest Service and was an outspoken voice for scientific forestry and the need to control and manage the country's natural resources. Grey Towers was more than the Pinchot home. Its grounds provided him with an opportunity to try many of his ideas on forestry. The first American school of forestry was held here for 21 years. The 3,000 acres enabled Pinchot to plant new forest land, and the area around the mansion provided Pinchot and his wife with an opportunity to put into practice their thoughts on the value of outdoor living.

Gifford and his wife, Cornelia Pinchot, made Grey Towers their permanent home in 1915. She realized that the mansion needed to be updated for use as a year-round

residence. The most significant interior changes involved major structural alterations. The original dining room and library had shared a central fireplace. Mrs. Pinchot had the fireplace and partition wall removed to create the present large dining room. She also transformed the billiard room and salon into a large library by removing another wall. While remodeling the house, she was also transforming the landscape. Hunt's original design for Grey Towers did not address the landscape. In a typical country estate, the mansion would dominate the site and the plantings would be kept away from the house. She created a new relationship between the indoors and outdoors with gardens and terraces near the main house to allow enjoyment of the outdoors and provide a seamless connection between the landscape and the house.

In 1963, Grey Towers was designated a National Historic Landmark and Gifford Bryce Pinchot, son of Gifford and Cornelia, donated Grey Towers and 102 acres to the US Forest Service. Assisted by the Grey Towers Heritage Association, the Forest Service works to carry on the Pinchot legacy by delivering public programs, interpretive tours, and conservation education programs. The site is used for conferences and seminars.

Drake Oil Well, see entry on opposite page.

Drake Oil Well

202 Museum Ln., Titusville; (814) 827-2797; drakewell.org; open weekends (Jan and Feb) and Tues through Sun (Mar through Dec); admission charged

Edwin L. Drake is credited with drilling the world's first oil well in the summer of 1859 in Titusville. In 1857 he traveled there as an agent of the Seneca Oil Company of New Haven with a directive to find crude oil that could be produced in quantities sufficient enough to be commercially successful. Reporting back that he felt confident this was possible, he went back in 1858 to begin the search for oil.

His biggest challenge was to find someone to work with near Titusville who didn't think he was crazy. Drake made the acquaintance of William (Uncle Billy) Smith who worked as a blacksmith and salt well driller. The two collaborated using Smith's experience in salt well drilling to develop a technology to drill for oil. After making several adjustments in the process, the work proceeded. The slow progress caused investors to pull out and "Drake's Folly" was in financial danger. Drake was forced to borrow money to continue work. On August 27, 1859, work stopped at a depth of 69.5 feet. Anticipating they would have to drill several hundred feet before reaching oil, Uncle Billy was surprised to find oil floating at the top of the pipe the next morning. News spread quickly throughout Titusville, and oil speculation soared. Drake is credited as the "father of the petroleum industry," because his technology changed the way crude oil was produced. For the next quarter of a century, Titusville was the center of oil production in the United States.

The Daughters of the American Revolution took the lead in preserving the site of Drake's oil well. They acquired the site and erected a monument dedicated in 1914. The Drake Well Museum and Park is owned by the Pennsylvania Historical and Museum Commission, in partnership with the Friends of Drake Well, Inc. The site includes an exact replica of Drake's engine house built around the oil well that was designated a National Historic Landmark in 1966. The original drilling site is also a National Historic Mechanical Engineering Landmark. The site includes a museum with a large artifact and archival collection on the birth of the modern petroleum industry.

Old West, Dickinson College,
see entry on p. 19.

Allegheny Portage Railroad of the Pennsylvania Canal
110 Federal Park Rd., Gallitzin; (814) 886-6150; nps.gov/alpo;
open year-round; no admission charged

Traveling across Pennsylvania in the early 1800s was a slow and difficult undertaking. In good conditions it took about 23 days to get from Philadelphia to Pittsburgh. After the completion of the Erie Canal in New York, Pennsylvania had to create a more efficient system for transportation to remain competitive. In 1826 the Pennsylvania legislature authorized the Mainline of Public Works to begin the building of canals from Philadelphia to Pittsburgh. The immediate problem was how to cross the Allegheny Mountain.

Modeled after a similar system in England, the 36-mile railroad was built consisting of 10 inclined planes, 5 on each side of the mountain. Five planes overcame the nearly 1,400-foot rise from Hollidaysburg on the east to the Allegheny Mountain summit at Blair's Gap; 5 more, including a 900-foot tunnel (see related entry on Staple Bend Tunnel), overcame the nearly 1,200-foot drop to Johnstown on the west. At the head of each inclined plane were two stationary engines that moved the endless rope to which the railroad cars were attached. Four cars, each capable of handling a 7,000-pound load, were drawn up at once and as many let down at the same time, and this operation could be performed from 6 to 10 times in one hour. The Allegheny Portage Railroad officially opened on March 18, 1834, and made it possible to travel from Philadelphia to Pittsburgh in four days. The Mainline of Public Works began an era of industrial prosperity in Pennsylvania.

During the early years of the railroad operation, passengers had to transfer from the canal boats to the railroad cars, then transfer successively at each plane and each

level of the railroad. Soon, an ingenious sectional boat system was developed, by which sections of canal boats could be loaded on railroad flat cars for transport over the mountains and then rejoined and floated down the remainder of the canal to their destination. Under this system, passengers could travel the entire route from Philadelphia to Pittsburgh without switching.

On February 15, 1854, the Pennsylvania Railroad completed the Horseshoe Curve, the final piece in a complete rail line from Philadelphia to Pittsburgh. The new rail line had no inclines and offered a continuous journey without the use of canals and the five switches needed to use the Mainline of Public Works. The Allegheny Portage Railroad ended operations in 1857 when the Pennsylvania Railroad purchased the canal system.

The Allegheny Portage Railroad was given National Historic Landmark status in 1962 and has been owned and operated as a unit of the National Park Service since 1964 as the Allegheny Portage Railroad National Historic Site. Visitors can tour the circa 1830 Lemon House, a tavern serving passengers on the railroad; Engine House No. 6 Exhibit Shelter, containing replica machinery as well as original foundations of the engine house; and the Skew Arch, a bridge built to accommodate the bend in the Huntingdon, Cambria and Indiana Turnpike.

Bedford Springs Hotel
2138 Business 220, Bedford; (814) 623-8100; omnihotels.com/ hotels/bedford-springs; open year-round; hotel tours offered daily; admission charged

During the 19th and early 20th centuries, wealthy Americans congregated at fashionable spas with natural mineral springs "taking the waters" for healing, cleansing, and rejuvenation. Bedford Springs was one of these well-known summer resorts. During the height of its popularity, Bedford Springs was a destination that offered not only rest and relaxation but a place to "see and be seen." James Buchanan spent 40 summers in Bedford Springs and used the resort as his summer White House during his term in office (1857–1861) (see related entry on James Buchanan House). In August 1858 Buchanan received the first transatlantic telegram in the lobby of the Bedford Springs Resort. It was from Queen Victoria congratulating him on the successful completion of this new method of communication. The message took 16 hours to send by Morse code through 2,500 miles of cable.

Mineral springs were used by the Native Americans for curing many ailments. Dr. John Anderson learned about the value of the springs for health and well-being from the Native Americans. He purchased 2,200 acres and built a house on the property, and as word spread of these unique waters, visitors arrived from around the globe to experience them. Visitors stayed in tents on the property, and Dr. Anderson

dispensed medical advice and prescriptions. In 1806 he built The Stone Inn to accommodate the increasing numbers of visitors.

The continued popularity of the destination spurred the construction of additional buildings and the development of new facilities and recreational activities. Six large, contiguous buildings of brick, wood, and stone dating from circa 1806 to circa 1903 comprise the main hotel complex and are excellent examples of Greek Revival, Italianate, Queen Anne/Eastlake, and Colonial Revival–style resort architecture. Following the Civil War, transportation and lodging improvements enticed an elite group of visitors to the site. In 1895 one of the first golf courses in the United States was laid out at Bedford Springs. One of the first indoor pools in the nation was constructed here in 1905, complete with a mineral water–fed swimming pool, solarium, and hydrotherapy rooms. In 1923 renowned golf course architect Donald Ross remodeled the 18-hole course.

Business suffered during the Depression, but World War II provided a new use for the facility. A naval radio training facility operated in the resort from 1941 to 1943. It then served as an internment camp for captured Japanese diplomats from 1943 to 1945. Postwar the resort resumed operations, and while it did not regain its former popularity, it was a destination for automobile tourists and a convention trade. Poor management decisions forced the hotel to close in 1986.

The property was designated a National Historic Landmark in 1991. It was purchased in 1998 and rehabilitated to its former glory. It reopened in 2007 as a hotel and spa and is operated by Omni Hotels and Resorts.

Carlisle Indian School
870 Jim Thorpe Rd., Carlisle Barracks; (717) 245-3721; armywarcollege.edu/ciis/index.cfm; open weekdays year-round; background check required to visit; no admission charged

In 1879 US Army Lieutenant Richard H. Pratt started a vocational training school with the purpose to eradicate traditional cultures so indigenous peoples could be accepted into white Western culture. He promoted the school as a place that would train thousands of Native people for careers and life among white culture. After serving in the Indian campaigns, he came to believe that the best approach for his students was to "civilize" them by removing them from their reservations and transporting them to the Carlisle Indian School (officially the Carlisle Indian Industrial School, or CIIS). The site selected was a former army cavalry base in Carlisle Barracks. While his ethnocentric approach was misguided, it presented an alternative to the government's policy of war against Native peoples and attempted to change the public's general hostility toward them.

Pratt visited the Dakota Territory and spoke with the elders of several reservations. He persuaded them to send their children to his school by convincing them that the continuing westward expansion would require them to be able to speak English and understand the ways of the white man if they wanted to be able to protect themselves and their property.

The school was a very structured military school. The day was divided into academics and trades. Students wore uniforms, marched in formation, and participated in regular drill practices. The goal was to fully assimilate these children in the ways of white American culture. Students spent their summers living and working in homes and on farms in Pennsylvania, Maryland, New York, Massachusetts, Ohio, and Virginia, practicing the trades and domestic skills they learned.

Enrollment grew from the original group of 82 to yearly averages of 1,000 students. The campus was enlarged, and several new buildings were constructed for additional classrooms and dormitories, a gymnasium, industrial training shops, a hospital, and a chapel. Music was an important part of the curriculum, and the school started a band that became quite well-known, performing at different events, including every presidential inaugural parade during the school's tenure.

Sports was also important and included track, baseball, football, basketball, and lacrosse, a traditional Native American game. The football team earned a national reputation, and although the school played against college teams and its athletes tended to be college-aged, CIIS was not a college. Its most famous athlete was Jim

Thorpe, who won gold medals for the pentathlon and decathlon at the 1912 Olympics. He went on to play professional baseball and football.

The school operated for 39 years, although Pratt left in 1904, and was attended by 8,000 Native children. Most returned to their reservations after leaving the school. The school closed in 1918, and the property was repurposed as a hospital for wounded World War I soldiers.

The Carlisle Indian School is a major site of memory for many Native people. It was designated a National Historic Landmark in 1961. The history is complex and includes many stories of the students who lived and died there. The former grounds of the school are located on the US Army War College. While the landscape has changed over the years, several school spaces, including the gymnasium, the superintendent's house, the farmhouse, and the cemetery, still exist. The cemetery was moved in the 1930s and no longer appears the way it did when the school was operating. Recently the farmhouse was designated as a Site of Conscience. Walking tour maps are available for purchase at the Cumberland County Historical Society.

Dwight D. Eisenhower Farm

1195 Baltimore Pike, Gettysburg; (717) 338-9114; nps.gov/eise;
open year-round; accessible only by shuttle bus from the Gettysburg
National Military Park Visitor Center; admission charged for shuttle

The 34th president of the United States, Dwight D. Eisenhower, was born in 1890
in Denison, Texas, the third of seven boys. All the boys were called Ike, intended as
an abbreviation of their last name, but only Dwight was still called Ike as an adult. In
1892 the family moved to Abilene, Kansas. He graduated from West Point in 1915
and married Mamie Doud in 1916, with whom he had two sons. During World
War I he was denied a request to serve in Europe and instead commanded Camp
Colt, the US Army Tank Corps Training Center, located on the fields of the Battle
of Gettysburg's famous Pickett's Charge.

Following World War I, he continued his service and was promoted to briga-
dier general in 1941. During World War II he supervised the D-Day invasions of
France and Germany. After the war he served as Army chief of staff before becoming
the president of Columbia University. Eisenhower had family roots in Pennsylvania
and remembered his days at Camp Colt fondly, so when the Eisenhowers began
searching for a retirement home in 1950, they purchased a farm adjoining the Gettysburg Battlefield. Retirement was delayed when Eisenhower assumed command of
the North Atlantic Treaty Organization (NATO) from 1951 to 1952. In 1952 he

launched his presidential bid, kicking off his Pennsylvania campaign by hosting state Republican leaders at a picnic at the farm.

While serving as president, he and Mrs. Eisenhower completely renovated their home in Gettysburg. When it was finished in March 1955, it was a modified Georgian farmhouse with eight bedrooms, nine bathrooms, a large living room, a formal dining room, a kitchen, a butler's pantry, and a glassed-in porch. The Eisenhowers used the house and farm on the weekends and holidays as an escape from the pressures of Washington, D.C., but early morning briefings kept the president up-to-date on world and domestic affairs. The farm served as a temporary White House in 1955 when Eisenhower was recovering from a heart attack. Eisenhower also ran a successful cattle business for 15 years at the farm. He invited world leaders to visit the house and farm, enjoying the informal setting of his porch to discuss issues.

After serving two terms as president, Eisenhower retired to the Gettysburg farm. He remained active in politics and enjoyed family life on the farm. The Eisenhowers donated their farm to the National Park Service in 1967. Two years later, Dwight "Ike" Eisenhower died at the age of 78. Mrs. Eisenhower remained at the farm until her death in 1979. The farm was designated a National Historic Landmark in 1966. The National Park Service opened the site in 1980.

The Eisenhower home retains most of its original furnishings and conveys the feeling that the occupants may have just stepped out of the house for a moment. Forty thousand artifacts are in the collection, including collectibles of the Eisenhower presidency that Mrs. Eisenhower enjoyed finding on their travels. At Christmas, the house is decorated with items they used each year.

East Broad Top Railroad
421 Meadow St., Rockhill; (814) 447-3011; febt.org; museum open first and third weekend of each month, May through Sept; no admission charged

The East Broad Top Railroad & Coal Co. (EBT) is a privately owned, regional, narrow-gauge railroad. It comprises 33 miles of track, chartered in 1856 and opened in 1873 and 1874. This railroad was established as a coal-carrying line in the heart of Pennsylvania's bituminous coal mining regions. In addition to coal, the line transported timber, sand, rock, general freight, and passengers. Instead of employing the standard width of 4 feet 8.5 inches between the rails, the East Broad Top's rails were separated by 3 feet. Narrow gauge was used at the time because the costs for grading was much less than standard gauge.

The property includes six narrow-gauge locomotives, built between 1911 and 1920, and a complete, belt-driven machine shop, foundry, and blacksmith shop, built between 1882 and 1933. The shops were used to build railroad cars, many of which

remain on the property. Common-carrier service ended in 1956. From 1960 until 2011, the EBT offered short, steam-powered tourist rides. Interpretive tours of the shop facilities are still offered to the general public.

Extraordinary for historical integrity, the East Broad Top Railroad is the most complete and original industrial historic site in the country, with buildings and machinery dating back over a century. It includes the oldest surviving narrow-gauge track in the United States. It was the last (of over 350) regional, narrow-gauge common-carrier railroads to operate east of the Rocky Mountains. Virtually all the surviving railroad equipment—including six narrow-gauge steam locomotives—was originally built for or by the EBT, and the machine tools used to do so are still on the property. It was designated a National Historic Landmark in 1964.

While the future of this resource remains uncertain, the Friends of the East Broad Top Railroad work to preserve and restore it. They operate a museum in Robertsdale that contains a collection of artifacts from the common carrier era. The Company Store offers modeling supplies for those who may wish to recreate the EBT in model form.

Horseshoe Curve

Veterans Memorial Hwy., Altoona; (814) 946-0834; railroadcity .com; open mid-Mar through mid-Nov; admission charged

In 1834 wagon transportation from Philadelphia to Pittsburgh took about 20 days. The same trip via train, canal, and the Allegheny Portage Railroad to cross the mountains (see related entry) took about four days when the canals weren't frozen or flooded. In 1838 a convention to urge the construction of a continuous railroad from Philadelphia to Pittsburgh assembled in Harrisburg and appointed Charles Schlatter to survey the route. He recommended a route that ran along the Juniata River in the east and the Conemaugh River in the west. By 1850 these two sections were the main route of the Pennsylvania Railroad's main line. Nevertheless, to cross the mountains, passengers and freight still depended on the slow and dangerous state-owned Allegheny Portage Railroad.

Chief engineer John Edgar Thomson designed the solution, which was to lay tracks so that the trains could cross the mountains directly. The route he chose proceeded west of Altoona, where it rose 122 feet at a practical grade of less than 2 percent, which a train of average length could manage with a helper locomotive. To construct this line, Thomson hired Irish laborers who lived in camps along the way and earned 25 cents an hour for a 12-hour day. They worked with the only tools available at that time—picks and shovels—to cut away the front of a mountain to form a ledge on which they could place the tracks. The soil and rocks that they removed were hauled in mule-drawn carts to fill two deep intervening ravines on each side of the center of the curve. The tracks went up the eastern side of the

mountain, turned left to cross the valleys to the western side, where they turned left again. The result resembled a horseshoe. The Horseshoe Curve over the mountain was placed in service in 1854. Passengers could now travel the entire route from Philadelphia to Pittsburgh in about 15 hours.

The rails' conquest of the mountains enabled the Pennsylvania Railroad to form alliances with other lines so that by the 1880s it had reached the Midwestern cities of Indianapolis, St. Louis, and Chicago. During the first half of the 1900s, the Horseshoe Curve was considered, along with the Panama Canal, the Empire State Building, and the Bay Bridge at San Francisco, one of the engineering "Wonders of the World."

In 1879 a park was dedicated to the engineering marvel at the bowl of the curve. In 1966 the curve was designated a National Historic Landmark. The park, a visitor center, and a funicular are operated by the Altoona Railroaders Memorial Museum. The line remains as busy as ever, usually hosting more than 50 Norfolk Southern freight trains and a few Amtrak passenger trains every day.

Leap-the-Dips, Lakemont Park
700 Park Ave., Altoona; (800) 434-8006; lakemontparkfun.com; open in the summer season; no admission charged for park; purchase ticket to ride

Leap-the-Dips, constructed in 1902, is the last known extant example of a side-friction figure-eight roller coaster in the country. The side-friction design was a

significant technological advancement in roller coaster design. It worked with two sets of wheels: normal road wheels and side-friction wheels designed to prevent cars from derailing on sharp curves. The roller coaster is located in Lakemont Park, originally developed by the Altoona and Logan Valley Electric Railway Company in the 1890s.

Lakemont Park was one of many "trolley parks" constructed by railway companies in the late 1800s and early 1900s to increase business on the weekends. During

the week passengers kept the trolleys full as they commuted to and from work; but on the weekend ridership, and revenue from collected fares, was low. The companies typically placed the parks at the ends of their lines to maximize use of the streetcars and to maximize their profits. In addition to building the parks, the railway companies typically owned and operated the parks. Often they also owned the electric utility in a community and would use the parks to showcase electricity by decorating them with many lights. Typically built near lakes, rivers, or beaches, the parks offered swimming along with bandstands, picnic groves, and ball fields. By 1919 there were as many as 1,000 trolley parks in the United States. Once the automobile grew in popularity, these trolley parks began to close. There are only 13 remaining trolley parks in the United States, 5 are in Pennsylvania, including Lakemont Park. The others are Bushkill Park in Easton, Dorney Park in Allentown, Kennywood Park in West Mifflin, and Waldameer Park in Erie.

Leap-the-Dips was built as an expansion to Lakemont Park. It was constructed almost completely out of wood with steel tracks. It is configured in a figure-eight design with gentle slopes. The ride is 1,452 feet long and 41 feet high, and cars travel about 10 miles per hour. By 1919 the side-friction coaster design was replaced by the under-friction roller coaster. It included a set of safety wheels that lock the cars to the track, now standard technology for wooden roller coasters.

Despite its outdated design, Leap-the-Dips operated continuously until 1985, when it closed after falling into disrepair. A fund-raising campaign led to its restoration in 1997 and a grand reopening in 1999. It was designated a National Historic Landmark in 1996 and received the Coaster Classic and Coaster Landmark Awards from American Coaster Enthusiasts. It is owned and operated by Lakemont Park.

Old West, Dickinson College
272 West High St., Carlisle; (717) 243-5121; dickinson.edu; exterior accessible year-round; contact for tours; no admission charged

Old West, the original building of Dickinson College, was designed by one of America's first professional architects, Benjamin Henry Latrobe. Latrobe was the second Architect of the Capitol, designed the porticos on the White House, and was responsible for many landmark buildings in Philadelphia. Designed in 1803 and built between 1803 and 1822, Old West still serves the college.

Dr. Benjamin Rush, a prominent Philadelphia physician, prepared the charter for Dickinson College in 1783. Rush had marched with the Continental Army, signed the Declaration of Independence, and served as a physician to the Philadelphia community. His intellect and progressive political thinking were critical in the

founding and growth of a young America. Rush believed that the only way for America to grow and thrive was to ensure that its citizens were well educated.

Rush asked John Dickinson, the governor of Pennsylvania, to lend his support and name to the college that was to be established in the "western frontier" of his state. Dickinson was known as the "Penman of the Revolution" for his twelve "Letters from a Farmer" published individually in 1767 and 1768. He was a member of the Continental Congress and wrote the first draft of the 1776–1777 Articles of Confederation and Perpetual Union.

The former Carlisle Grammar School served as the first college building, but was soon too small to accommodate the growing student population. Construction began on a new building in 1799, but it was destroyed by fire in 1803 before it was finished.

The college trustees appealed to Benjamin Latrobe for help with the reconstruction of the burned building. He agreed and designed Old West free of charge. With donations from Thomas Jefferson, James Madison, Aaron Burr, and others, the cornerstone at Old West was placed on August 8, 1803. The building hosted its first classes in 1805. The building was completed in 1822.

The building is three stories high, built of limestone quarried near Carlisle, with local red sandstone used for the trim. It has a central pedimented projection with a two-story arched opening, flanked by sidelights and topped by an elegant fanlight, a signature feature of the Federal style. The roof is topped with an open cupola. The mermaid weathervane that tops the cupola has become the college's symbol. Although much of the interior has been altered to serve modern needs, the old chapel, now Memorial Hall, remains one of the most delicately elaborate and beautiful rooms of the Federal period.

In 1962 Old West was designated a National Historic Landmark, and it now serves as the home of administrative offices and classrooms, while continuing to be the center of Dickinson's campus.

Interior of Beth
Sholom Synagogue,
see entry on p. 35

SOUTHEAST

1762 Waterworks
Visitor Center, 505 Main St., Bethlehem; (800) 360-8687; historicbethlehem.org; open year-round; downloadable trail tour or audio tour available; fee charged for tour material

Bethlehem was settled in 1741 as the first successfully established community of German Moravians in North America. The Moravians lived in a communal society organized into groups, called choirs, and segregated by age, gender, and marital status. Moravians worked together and provided for the good of the community. Buildings associated with the Moravian community in Bethlehem are built in the German Colonial style of architecture.

Many of its earliest buildings are still extant, including the 1762 Waterworks, designated a National Historic Landmark in 1981. The two-and-one-half-story limestone structure, topped by a red tile roof, housed the mechanical system for pumping water from a nearby spring. This system is believed to be the first pump-powered

water supply in the United States. (Boston, Massachusetts, had a municipal water supply as early as 1652, but it was powered by gravity.) The earliest portions of the water supply date from 1755. The pump house was constructed in 1762 with an 18-foot-diameter undershot waterwheel that powered cast-iron pumps to force water from the spring up 94 vertical feet to a tower. By gravity, the tower fed five cisterns throughout the town. The Waterworks was actively used as a pumping station until the 1830s, although the spring remained the main water source for Bethlehem until the early 20th century.

In addition to its National Historic Landmark status, the Waterworks is a Historic Civil Engineering Landmark and an American Water Landmark. The Waterworks is located within the Historic Moravian Bethlehem Historic District, a National Historic Landmark District designated in 2012. It is owned and operated as a historic site by Historic Bethlehem Museums and Sites. It can be viewed along the 1-mile Historic Bethlehem Moravian Founders Heritage Trail that focuses on the settlement of the city by the Moravians and the building of its prosperous economy.

Academy of Music
240 S. Broad St., Philadelphia; (215) 893-1999; academyofmusic .org; open year-round for ticketed performances; admission charged

The Academy of Music, built as an opera house, has been in continuous use since its opening in 1857. Beginning with a performance of Verdi's Il trovatore, this venue has featured an impressive list of dignitaries and performers. In 1870 Susan B. Anthony campaigned for a woman's right to vote, and President Ulysses S. Grant accepted his nomination for a second term during the Republican National Convention in 1872. With the main-level seats covered by a wooden stage, the Academy hosted a circus with Buffalo Bill Cody in 1873. In 1891 Peter Tchaikovsky conducted music from *The Nutcracker.*

The Academy was designed in the Renaissance Revival style and features facades of brownstone with brick trim. The Broad Street elevation is dominated by five large arched windows above arched entrances below. The interior, with its columned proscenium and tiers of boxes, is regarded as a very early American example of the Neo-Baroque style. The auditorium was designed in an oval shape with its massive Corinthian columns placed in sections so that every seat in the space could see the stage without obstruction. It included four stacked balconies and a massive crystal chandelier that came from the Crystal Palace in New York City. The auditorium, while very ornate with its intricate painted ceiling and brilliant red, gold, and cream furnishings, still conveys an intimate feeling that connects the audience with the performers.

Although built as an opera house, the Academy was home to the Philadelphia Orchestra from 1900 to 2001. The Orchestra established itself as one of the world's greatest, with a vast number of premieres and the legendary "Philadelphia Sound," under the leadership of conductor Leopold Anthony Stokowski, who served as conductor from 1912 to 1941. Stokowski was the first conductor in the industry to become a true superstar. He appeared in several films but is most famous for his role in Walt Disney's *Fantasia* as the orchestra leader who talks to Mickey Mouse. During "The Sorcerer's Apprentice," Mickey Mouse dreams that he can control nature with his hands and mimics Stokowski's gestures conducting the orchestra. Stokowski convinced Walt Disney to record the music of *Fantasia* in Philadelphia with the Philadelphia Orchestra at the Academy of Music in 1939. It took 42 days and 90 miles of film to record.

The Academy of Music is an active theater with a full season of shows each year, some performed by the resident companies including Opera Philadelphia, the Pennsylvania Ballet, and the Philly Pops, in addition to several touring companies. The Academy of Music is currently owned by the Philadelphia Orchestra Association and managed by Kimmel Center, Inc. The Academy of Music Restoration Fund, a separate nonprofit, oversees the long-term preservation of this National Historic Landmark, designated in 1962.

Alfred Newton Richards Medical Research Laboratories and David Goddard Laboratories Building, University of Pennsylvania
3700 Hamilton Walk, Philadelphia; (215) 898-2876; facilities .upenn.edu; exterior accessible year-round; no admission charged

The Alfred Newton Richards Medical Research Laboratories and the David Goddard Laboratories are two connected laboratory and classroom buildings on the campus of the University of Pennsylvania. Although they were completed at different times and served different departments, they were a single design project by architect Louis Kahn.

Louis I. Kahn was born in Estonia and migrated with his family to Philadelphia in 1906. He earned his degree in architecture from the University of Pennsylvania in 1924. He was progressive in his ideas, studying the modern designs of European architects. Kahn believed that buildings should convey their weight and their method of construction. His designs were powerful with an emphasis on masonry materials. One of his main interests was in the design of public housing in the 1950s. Many of his progressive designs were never built, but they are a fascinating study of his ideas. Kahn's teaching career began in 1947 with an appointment at Yale. In 1955 he returned to the University of Pennsylvania as a teacher.

The Richards and Goddard Research Laboratories project began in 1957 when Kahn was awarded the commission. Construction was substantially completed by the end of 1963, with landscape work and final documentation finished in 1965. The buildings continue to serve their original program purposes, that is, the Richards Building is occupied by research laboratories, while the Goddard Building houses research and teaching laboratories, offices, and classrooms as it was originally designed to do. The buildings are named in honor of two University of Pennsylvania professors and scientists: The Richards Medical Research Laboratory named for Alfred Newton Richards (1876–1966) in 1960 and the David Goddard Laboratories renamed for David Rockwell Goddard (1908–1985) in 1983.

The buildings consist of a series of flat-roofed connected towers, most of which are square in plan, and vary in height from six to nine stories above grade. The principal exterior materials are exposed reinforced concrete and red brick, with steel-frame fixed-sash windows. Three eight-story towers arranged like a pinwheel attached to a fourth tower comprise the Richards Research laboratories. The laboratories are located within the three spokes of the pinwheel, and the fourth tower is used for mechanical systems and vertical access by elevator or stairs. The Goddard Building has two towers with laboratories and a third tower for mechanicals and access. The towers are in a straight line and connect to the Richards building. A research library in the Goddard Building's upper floors feature reading carrels that cantilever from the building's face.

Considered one of Kahn's most important works of the mid-20th century, it brought broad international recognition to him. The Salk Institute in California (1965) and the Kimbell Art Museum in Texas (1972) were masterpieces completed late in his career. He died in 1974 at the age of 73.

The buildings are owned by the University of Pennsylvania. They were designated National Historic Landmarks in 2009.

American Philosophical Society Hall
104 S. Fifth St., Philadelphia; (215) 440-3440; amphilsoc.org; open mid-Apr through Dec, Thurs through Sun; admission charged

The American Philosophical Society, the oldest learned society in the United States, was founded in 1743 by Benjamin Franklin to "promote useful knowledge." Early members included doctors, lawyers, clergymen, and merchants interested in science, and learned artisans and tradesmen like Franklin. Many founders of the republic were members, including George Washington, John Adams, Thomas Jefferson, Alexander Hamilton, Thomas Paine, Benjamin Rush, and James Madison, as well as many distinguished foreigners, including Lafayette and von Steuben.

The study of nature, including astronomy, was an important pursuit in the 1760s, and the members of the American Philosophical Society used this study as a means to find ways to improve the practice of agriculture, manufacturing, and transportation to gain economic independence for America. With one of his telescopes, erected on a platform behind the State House (now Independence Hall), David Rittenhouse plotted the transit of Venus and gained the recognition of the scholarly world, and by 1769 the Society had international acclaim for this work.

The construction of the American Philosophical Hall as a permanent home for the Society was first conceived in 1769, but it was not implemented until 1785 when the Pennsylvania Assembly awarded the Society a lot on Independence Square behind Independence Hall. The digging of the cellar was begun in 1785, but the building slowed with the lag in subscription funds. Finally, with considerable aid from Benjamin Franklin, the Hall was completed and housed its first meeting in 1789. The two-and-a-half-story rectangular brick building was built in the Late Georgian style with a raised basement and a hip roof with two gabled dormers facing on both the east and west. The central doorways on the eastern and western facades consist of two paneled pilasters supporting a round arch over a basket-weave fanlight.

In 1890, to provide additional space, the original hip roof and its deck were replaced by a flat-roofed, brick third story. This was removed in 1946 to restore the Hall to its historic appearance, and the document collection was relocated. The library is now housed directly across Fifth Street in a replica of the Library Company building that formerly faced the Hall. The Library Company of Philadelphia, also founded by Benjamin Franklin, is now located on Locust Street.

The American Philosophical Society owns and occupies the building, designated a National Historic Landmark in 1965. It serves as a museum and administrative offices. The Society continues to fulfill its original mission by engaging leading scholars, scientists, and professionals through an elected membership. Scholars from around the world use the research library, which is filled with historic manuscripts. The membership continues to support scholarly research with grants, lectures, publications, and annual prizes. Current membership is approximately 1,000 and includes both citizens of the United States and international members.

Andalusia
1237 State Rd., Andalusia; (215) 245-5479; andalusiapa.org; open Apr through Oct; tour reservations required; admission charged

One of the finest examples of the Greek Revival style in the United States, Andalusia is associated with the life of Nicholas Biddle, a financier who as president of the Second Bank of the United States (see related entry) made it the first effective central bank in US history. Originally built in 1797 as a summer home by John Craig, a wealthy shipping merchant, the house was enlarged in 1806 under the direction of Benjamin Latrobe, known as the country's first professional architect. Some of Latrobe's buildings included the Bank of the United States in Philadelphia and the US Capitol in Washington, D.C.

A child prodigy, Nicholas Biddle completed his studies at the University of Pennsylvania at age 13. His parents then sent him to the College of New Jersey (now Princeton University), where he graduated at age 15 and gave the valedictory speech at graduation. He read law in the office of his older brother and was admitted to the bar in 1809. Biddle's association with Andalusia began with his marriage to Jane Craig in 1811. In 1819 he was appointed as one of the directors of the Second Bank of the

United States, and was elected president of the bank in 1823. Under Biddle's leadership, the once-shaky institution came to control state banks, regulate currency, and protect the commercial operations of the nation. Unhappy with the firm regulations implemented by Biddle, Andrew Jackson vetoed the bill to recharter the bank in 1832. Biddle retired to Andalusia and pursued other interests.

Andalusia strongly reflects the interests of Nicholas Biddle. In 1833 he commissioned Thomas Ustick Walter, who later worked on the US Capitol, to add a south wing to the existing house that showcased Biddle's long affection for classical Greek architecture. The new wing resembled a Greek temple with six Doric columns in the front facing the Delaware River. This was oriented in the opposite direction from the original front and now appears as the main facade of the building.

The interior of the house has changed very little, including the furniture, most of which dates to Biddle's era. Of special interest is the library, a room added in 1834, that still contains its original bookcases and more than 3,000 rare volumes, some dating to the 17th century.

In 1980 James Biddle, Nicholas's great-great-grandson, then president of the National Trust for Historic Preservation and a leader of the historic preservation movement in the United States, made the decision to divide Andalusia and give away the house and nearly 50 acres of land to the Andalusia Foundation. The time had come, he felt, to share Andalusia's beauty with others who would understand and appreciate it just as the Biddle family had done for generations. Andalusia was designated a National Historic Landmark in 1966 and is owned and operated by the Andalusia Foundation.

Andrew Wyeth Studio and Kuerner Farm
1821 S. Creek Rd. and 325 Ring Rd., Chadds Ford; (610) 388-2700; brandywine.org; access only via shuttle from the Brandywine River Museum of Art (1 Hoffman's Mill Rd., Chadds Ford); guided tours Apr through Nov; admission charged

Andrew Newell Wyeth was born in 1917 in Chadds Ford. By the time of Andrew's birth, his father, N. C. Wyeth, was a renowned and well-published illustrator of Western stories, historical narratives, and novels such as *Treasure Island* and *Kidnapped* (see related entry). Andrew was the youngest of five children in a remarkably talented family that included several painters, a composer, and a scientist. Considered one of the greatest artists of the 20th century, Andrew Wyeth was primarily a realist painter. His favorite subjects were the land and people around him, both around his hometown of Chadds Ford and his summer home in mid-coast Maine.

Wyeth wandered the countryside near Chadds Ford as a boy. Very early he found the Kuerner farm to the east of his family's house. He was welcomed at the farm and permitted to explore the property. He was fascinated by German farmers Karl and Anna Kuerner. The young Wyeth was captivated by the farm, the methods of farming, and especially by the people and their traditions that he came to know well. As a teenager, Andrew Wyeth made oil paintings and drawings at the farm. Those early years established ties between the artist and the place, and between the artist and the Kuerner family that would last throughout their lives. When in Pennsylvania he always drew and painted on the farm.

Andrew Wyeth formally entered his father's studio in 1932 at the age of 15. As he progressed in his studies, Andrew rebelled against his father's strict teaching. To escape, he painted outdoors in the surrounding countryside, depicting the places and views that would become familiar icons in his work. By 1940 Andrew had repurposed a schoolhouse, originally built in 1875, for his studio. It was near his father's studio and a short distance from Kuerner Farm. For nearly 60 years he spent every fall and winter in Chadds Ford. Inspired by the landscape and people there, Wyeth created thousands of paintings and drawings in his studio. After Andrew married, he and his wife Betsy divided their time between Cushing, Maine, where they spent summers, and Chadds Ford.

After the death of Karl and Anna Kuerner, their son arranged for the Brandywine Conservancy, Inc., to purchase a portion of the Kuerner Farm. In 1998 he donated the remainder of the estate. Betsy James Wyeth donated Andrew's studio to the Conservancy after Andrew's death in 2009. The studio contains original furnishings, arts supplies, books, and collections and conveys the feeling that the artist has just stepped out for a moment. Now Kuerner Farm and the Andrew Wyeth Studio are managed by the Brandywine River Museum of Art. Both properties were designated National Historic Landmarks in 2011.

Arch Street Friends Meeting House

320 Arch St., Philadelphia; (215) 413-1804; historicasmh.org; open June through Oct, Tues through Sat; other times by appointment; admission charged

The Religious Society of Friends (Quakers) embrace the ideals of simplicity, plainness, and equality. The Quaker building tradition is reflected in simple designs, high-quality materials, and good craftsmanship. Meetinghouses reflect those values and the Arch Street Meeting House is no exception. Since worship involves silent contemplation without clergy or ritual, there is no need for an altar or a pulpit. Meeting spaces are simple rooms with natural light on the ground level with a second-floor gallery. Wooden benches provide the seating.

In 1701 the land was deeded to the Society of Friends by William Penn for use as a burial ground, though burials took place there as early as 1683. The burial ground was mostly full by the time of the meetinghouse's construction. As part of their ideal of simplicity, the Quakers in Philadelphia did not use headstones, and the remains were largely left in the ground during construction of the meetinghouse. The last burial took place in 1880.

The Arch Street Meeting House was designed in 1803 and 1804 by Quaker Owen Biddle Jr., who planned for the building to contain three main rooms. The east room and central meeting space were built in 1804, and the west room followed in 1811. The Georgian-style brick building is simple yet elegant in design, with original multiple-pane double hung windows and columned porticos at each entrance. The building has been expanded many times over the years but still retains its Colonial-era appearance. The building has several meeting spaces, all very simple and in the traditional style with wooden benches, natural light, and second-floor galleries.

The property has been continuously and actively used since 1682. The Arch Street Meeting House is open for tours, meetings, and community functions and is the location of the Monthly Meeting of the Friends of Philadelphia. In 2011 the Arch Street Meeting House became a National Historic Landmark and the Arch Street Meeting House Preservation Trust was formed. The Trust preserves, operates, and interprets the meetinghouse and grounds while serving the community and increasing public understanding of the impact and continued relevance of Quakers and Quaker history.

Athenaeum
219 S. Sixth St., Philadelphia; (215) 925-2688; philaathenaeum .org; open weekdays year-round; no admission charged

According to the Mission Statement of the Athenaeum of Philadelphia, the Athenaeum was founded in 1814 to collect items "connected with the history and antiquities of America, and the useful arts, and generally to disseminate useful knowledge for public benefit." After 30 years of sharing quarters with the Philosophical Society, the members of the Athenaeum held a design competition for its new headquarters. Architect John Notman was selected over the designs submitted by William Stickland, John Haviland, and Thomas U. Walter, all very prolific and well-known architects in Philadelphia.

Built between 1845 and 1847, the Athenaeum is one of the first Italian Renaissance Revival buildings in the United States. Notman's innovative use of brownstone (one of the first uses of this material in Philadelphia) led to its widespread popularity across the United States. Winning this commission helped the architect gain a reputation as one of the leading architects of his time. The Athenaeum is considered one of the most significant American buildings of the 19th century. The design was published widely in other cities and often copied. The use of brownstone as both wall and trim material results in the building appearing rather plain, at first

glance, but its rich detail is remarkable. The interior contains richly embellished reading rooms with grained woodwork, marbled columns, and original gas lighting fixtures. These spaces contain a notable collection of paintings, statuary, and period furniture. The Athenaeum was one of the first institutions to take an active interest in American Empire decorative arts.

As its collections expanded, other societies were founded to become caretakers of historic materials. The Historical Society of Pennsylvania and the Franklin Institute both grew out of the Athenaeum's membership. This allowed the Athenaeum to refine its focus as an independent member-supported library and museum. Thousands of researchers, scholars, architects, interior designers, museum curators, and historic property owners use the collection of the Athenaeum, which focuses on American architecture and building technology and includes 180,000 architectural drawings, more than 350,000 photographs, and the records of 1,000 American architects. The bulk of the collection is available digitally.

The building was designated a National Historic Landmark in 1976. The Athenaeum is an excellent steward of its impressive collections and beautiful headquarters.

Augustus Lutheran Church
717 W. Main St., Trappe; (610) 489-9625; augustustrappe.org; exterior accessible year-round; contact for service schedule; no admission charged

In 1717 German Lutheran immigrants settled in the area now known as Trappe in Montgomery County. They worshipped under the care of itinerant preachers, but prayed for a leader to guide them. Reverend Henry Melchior Muhlenberg arrived from Germany in 1742, and by 1743 his congregation began building the Augustus Lutheran Church. Dedicated in September 1745, this distinctive structure with its polygonal apse and gambrel roof is one of the country's best examples of vernacular German ecclesiastical architecture.

The exterior walls, made of local sandstone, have been plastered, and the original gambrel roof of wooden shingles has undergone several replacements, but the integrity of the structure is intact. Very few changes have been made on the interior. There are galleries on three sides, two that date from 1742 and feature a cut-out railing with heart-shaped figures. The paneled walnut pulpit, which serves as a focal point, was received in 1745 as a gift from English church members. The northeast loft was built in 1752 to accommodate a new organ imported from Europe. All the pews are original. Those beneath the organ loft were for the elders; those beneath the western gallery, with carved doors and elaborate locks, were for the wealthier members of the congregation. As was customary in the colonial period, the sexes were separated.

The church was used as a field hospital by the Continental Army during the Revolutionary War. Muhlenberg served as pastor until his death in 1787. The congregation continued to grow, and by 1852 a larger church was needed. A second church, known as "the Brick Church," serves as the main sanctuary of the Augustus Lutheran Church. The original church, known as the "Old Trappe Church," was reserved for special occasions. A portion of the Old Trappe Church's roof was destroyed by a windstorm in 1860, and the congregation considered demolishing the original church building. Muhlenberg's great-grandson, Reverend William Augustus Muhlenberg, an Episcopal minister, stepped in to help raise funds to restore the building.

The Augustus Lutheran Church has an active congregation who are committed to the preservation of the "Old Trappe Church." It is a testament to the founders of the church and is the oldest, unchanged Lutheran Church building in continuous use in the United States. Services are held in the original church through the summer, on Christmas Eve, and on special occasions. The original church was designated a National Historic Landmark in 1967.

Beth Sholom Synagogue
8231 Old York Rd., Elkins Park; (215) 887-1342; bethsholompreservation.org; guided tours available; admission charged

Constructed between 1954 and 1959, Beth Sholom Synagogue has been recognized as one of architect Frank Lloyd Wright's most important commissions. Wright designed only a small number of religious buildings, and Beth Sholom is his only

synagogue. It is one of only 16 Wright buildings singled out in 1959 by the American Institute of Architects and the National Trust for Historic Preservation as buildings that should be preserved in their original form. The mission of the Beth Sholom Synagogue Preservation Foundation is to preserve the building, furniture, and landscape setting to the highest standards possible to tell the story of this great American synagogue. Beth Sholom was designated a National Historic Landmark in 2007.

The Beth Sholom Congregation, a Conservative Jewish congregation, was founded in 1918 in Philadelphia and named "house of peace" (the meaning of the Hebrew name) in honor of the end of World War I. In 1953 Rabbi Mortimer Cohen persuaded Wright to accept the commission for a synagogue in the congregation's new location in Elkins Park. Rabbi Cohen's first letter established the working relationship between the clergyman and the architect, specifically that the rabbi would take the lead in explaining and interpreting Jewish practices and beliefs as Wright proceeded with the building's design. Wright and the Rabbi developed a close working relationship, and their correspondence indicates that Wright's reputation of telling clients what they want was not the case in this commission. Wright's initial scheme for the entrance canopy was very modest. Rabbi Cohen suggested it should instead represent the hands of the ancient priests, outstretched in blessing. He directed Wright to imagine his two hands together in prayer, then to pivot them on the thumb and first finger, revolving them up until both hands are in one plane, creating a triangular shape. Wright changed the design and that canopy design welcomes visitors today. The synagogue was dedicated in September 1959, just five months after Wright's death.

The synagogue is a striking geometric building with a two-part design: a glass pyramidal tower that rises from a hexagonal base. The elevations come to a point facing east, orienting the worshippers to the arks (the receptacles that hold the Torah scrolls) placed near the building's eastern point, facing in the direction of Jerusalem. Both the exterior and interior are organized on repeating motifs of triangular and hexagonal forms representing tents and mountains. Lamps resembling menorahs embellish the west sides of the northwest and southwest projections. The upper portion of the building is topped by an aluminum finish cap, which continues the decorative motif of the other metal portions of the exterior. The distinctive two-part exterior is visible on the interior of the building as well. The upper pyramidal tower houses the main sanctuary. The base of the building contains a smaller sanctuary and spaces for social activities. Virtually all the original Wright-designed details survive unaltered, from the room divisions, finishes, light fixtures, furniture, colors, flooring, and trim.

Boathouse Row
1 Boathouse Row, Philadelphia; (215) 685-3936; boathouserow.org; exterior accessible year-round; no admission charged

Situated on the bank of the Schuylkill River, Boathouse Row is one of the most photographed sites in Philadelphia, especially at night when each of the private club-houses are outlined in lights. When the houses were first lit in the 1970s, the lights were incandescent and they twinkled. Now the lights are LED and the colors can be changed for the seasons and special events.

The Schuylkill River was a center of recreation for Philadelphia residents from its earliest times, a popular place for swimming and fishing. In the early 19th century, the Fairmount Water Works and Fairmount Dam altered the river from a tidal stream to a very long freshwater lake. It provided a calm surface, ideal for skaters when frozen. Skating was so popular that in 1849 the Philadelphia Skating Club formed to promote the sport and to rescue skaters in danger. This section of the river was also one of the finest places in the United States for the new sport of rowing.

In 1855 Philadelphia formed Fairmount Park using the Lemon Hill Estate, purchased in 1844, that extended to the bank of the river. Several boathouses had been erected along the river, but they were poorly built and the city condemned them in 1859. The city allowed the erection of three stone boathouses and the stone Skating Club in 1860. Between 1867 and 1904, 11 more boathouses were built, the earliest ones in the Victorian Gothic style. Some of the boathouses were enlarged and combined over time, resulting in a total of 12 boathouses remaining. While each boathouse is unique with an interesting story, there are few of note. Considered to be one of the best architecturally is the Undine Club (#13), designed by Frank Furness (Furness and Evans) built in 1882 and 1883. The Philadelphia Girls Rowing Club, composed primarily of wives of oarsmen who wished to participate in a mostly all-male sport, was organized in 1938 and owns the former Philadelphia Skating Club (#14). It is the oldest active women's club in existence. The Bachelors Barge Club (#6) is the oldest continuously operating rowing organization in the United States, dating back to 1853.

The Schuylkill Navy, formed in 1858, is an association of amateur rowing clubs. It is the oldest amateur athletic governing body in the United States, and its rules have helped clarify distinctions between amateur and professional sports throughout the country. Each of the boathouses is still part of the Schuylkill Navy. Of the 12 rowing clubs that occupy Boathouse Row, several are still active in the sport of rowing and providing space for high school and college rowing teams to practice. Boathouse Row was designated a National Historic Landmark in 1987.

Brandywine Battlefield
1491 Baltimore Pike, Chadds Ford; (610) 459-3342; brandywinebattlefield.org; open Mar through Dec, hours vary; no admission charged

On September 11, 1777, General George Washington was determined to prevent the British from capturing Philadelphia, the American seat of government. Taking up positions along the Brandywine Creek, Washington mistakenly believed that his army blocked all fords across the Brandywine. General William Howe and an army

of 15,500 British Regulars and Hessian troops were making their way to Philadelphia from the south.

The Hessians were ordered to confront the Americans at Chadds Ford, while General Howe's troops crossed the Brandywine farther upstream. The battle with the Hessians had been going on for hours when Howe's forces appeared undetected on the Continentals' right flank. Washington dispatched troops to defend his flank but was unsuccessful. The Hessians continued their battle from the front and eventually Washington's line collapsed. Washington ordered one of his divisions to protect the rear so the Continental Army could escape to the northwest. The counterattack continued until nightfall when the remaining Americans retreated, led by a wounded Marquis de Lafayette.

The Continental Army demonstrated a newly won ability to withstand the determined attack of British regulars, even while sustaining heavy losses. However, the American defeat led to the British occupation of Philadelphia on September 26, 1777. Even though the battle was a British victory and achieved the goal of taking Philadelphia, General Howe was criticized for not destroying the Continental Army. A few months later he was relieved of his command and replaced by General Henry Clinton.

A commemorative park was established in 1949 by the Commonwealth of Pennsylvania. The Brandywine Battlefield National Historic Landmark contains 50 square miles of land and includes 15 municipalities in 2 counties. Visitors to the battlefield can tour the Benjamin Ring House that served as Washington's Headquarters and the Gideon Gilpen House where Lafayette stayed briefly. The Gilpen house was also plundered by foraging soldiers after the battle. Gilpen ran a tavern out of his home to help support his family following the devastation of his farm. Brandywine Battlefield Park is administered by the Pennsylvania Historical and Museum Commission (PHMC) in partnership with the Brandywine Battlefield Park Associates, leading the interpretation and preservation of this National Historic Landmark, designated in 1961.

Carpenters' Hall
320 Chestnut St., Philadelphia; (215) 925-0167; carpentershall .org; open year-round, closed Mon (and Tues in Jan and Feb); no admission charged

The Carpenters' Company of the City and County of Philadelphia, probably the oldest builder's organization in the United States, was founded in 1724. Modeled after trade guilds of England, the most famous of which is "Worshipful Company of Carpenters' of London," its members were primarily master builders, making the name a bit of a misnomer. Master builders fulfilled the duties of both architect and contractor, and members of the Carpenters' Company were responsible for much of the design and construction of Philadelphia.

Carpenters' Hall, erected in 1770 to 1774, is a fine example of late-Georgian architecture. It is constructed of brick, with two central pedimented pavilions on the north and south sides giving the structure a Greek cross plan. The roof is crowned with an octagonal cupola. The north entrance has broad high steps leading to a

pedimented double doorway with a fanlight above. This decorative wooden door with engaged Doric columns was installed in 1791 to finally complete the building.

In 1773, before the building was completed, Benjamin Franklin moved his Library Company, the first free-lending library, into the building where it remained for 17 years. The First Continental Congress met here in 1774 and listed the grievances of the colonies, demanding that the King of England and Parliament address these concerns. It served as an infirmary, first for American, then British, officers from 1776 to 1778, and the War Office used the Hall as an arsenal from 1778 to 1779. Beginning in 1780 the American Philosophical Society used the building as a meeting place for five years until their own building was completed. The Bank of North America, a private bank, occupied the first floor from 1791 to 1793. It served as temporary offices for both the First and Second Bank of the United States until each of their headquarters was completed. The Philadelphia Customs House was located in the Hall from 1801 to 1817. In 1821 the Philadelphia College of Pharmacy was established here. The Carpenters' Company school of architecture, one of the nation's first, began holding classes here in 1833.

After some concern over the use of the building as an auction house between 1828 and 1857, the Company decided to terminate the lease and renovate the Hall. It was opened to the public in 1857. The building is privately owned, open for tours, and located within the boundaries of Independence National Historical Park. It was designated a National Historic Landmark in 1970. It still serves the original purpose: a meeting place for the Carpenters' Company.

Christ Church

20 North American St., Philadelphia; (215) 922-1695; christchurchphila.org; open year-round except Mon and Tues in Jan and Feb and during services; no admission charged

Established in 1695 by members of the Church of England, Christ Church was the birthplace of the American Episcopal Church. The first church was a simple wood building on the present site. The current church was constructed between 1727 and 1744. Its steeple, 196 feet in height, was added in 1754 and financed by a lottery organized by Benjamin Franklin. For 56 years it was the tallest structure in North America.

Known as "The Nation's Church," the congregation included Presidents George Washington and John Adams, Betsy Ross, John Penn (grandson of William Penn), and 15 signers of the Declaration of Independence, including Benjamin Franklin and Benjamin Rush. Brass plaques mark the pews where these individuals sat.

Its association with the early leaders of the United States is important, but Christ Church is best known for its striking architecture. It is one of the finest examples of Georgian architecture in the United States, with an elegance that is unmatched in other 18th-century churches. The main portion of the building is two stories in height with brick walls laid in a Flemish bond pattern with glazed headers. A prominent feature of the building is its massive Palladian window on the eastern facade that provides light to the interior of the sanctuary. On the opposite elevation

is a square brick tower topped by the tall octagonal wooden steeple. The steeple was repaired in 1771 and rebuilt in its original form after a fire in 1908.

The interior is dominated by pairs of fluted Doric columns that support lateral arches and an elliptical plaster ceiling. The chancel is located within an elliptical arch that frames the Palladian window. The branched chandelier, above the center aisle of the church, was installed in 1744 and is still hanging in its original place. The baptismal font in which William Penn was baptized is still in use, sent to Philadelphia in 1697 by the All Hallows by the Tower Church in London. The wine-glass pulpit, the reading desk, and a second baptismal font were made in 1770.

Christ Church is famous for its "Chime of Eight Bells" that were rung after the Declaration of Independence was read to the public on July 8, 1776. It was feared the bells would be confiscated by the British, so they were taken down in 1777 and returned in 1778 after the British evacuated Philadelphia. The bells are rung each year on July 4.

The burial ground, located at the intersection of Fifth and Arch Streets, is a unique Colonial-era graveyard with 1,400 markers on two acres. It is the final resting place for many prominent early leaders, including Benjamin Franklin.

Christ Church is privately owned with an active Episcopal congregation and is an important historic site within Independence National Historical Park. It was declared a National Historic Landmark in 1970.

Church of the Advocate

1801 W. Diamond St., Philadelphia; (215) 978-8000; churchoftheadvocate.org; open year-round; tours by appointment; no admission charged

Built as a memorial to merchant and civic leader George W. South, the Church of the Advocate was financed by the private philanthropy of his family, who after his death wanted to erect and endow a church in an area where there was the greatest need. They selected the rapidly developing neighborhood of North Philadelphia.

Between 1887 and 1897 a sprawling complex of buildings, designed to suggest a medieval compound, was constructed in a high-style Gothic Revival design. Notably, the buildings are not oriented with the traditional street grid of the neighborhood. The cruciform shape of the church is situated at an angle on the lot so that the church faces true east, a tradition that allowed Christians to pray eastward. Of architectural interest is the semicircular apse with its flying buttresses on the east elevation and the polygonal narthex that projects from the body of the church on the west elevation, dominated by a large rose-shaped stained-glass window. Carved faces and grotesques are fun to spot on all sides of the building.

Most impressive are the stone carvings throughout the interior, including carved busts of saints and apostles, as well as portraits of people connected with the church.

Three heads of cherubs, peeking from behind the wings of angels, are accented by a continuous frieze of cherubs with crossed wings. The carved lectern is especially noteworthy, showing a saint reading a book between two saints wielding double-edged swords and surrounded by the lion, ox, eagle, and angel representing the four evangelists, Matthew, Mark, Luke, and John.

The socially conscious goals of the church's founders who specified that the church should be "free for all time" continue. By choosing this neighborhood with its

working-class population, the Souths demonstrated that community mission work was as important as architectural splendor. However, this mixing of social philanthropy and architectural ambition taxed the limits of the $50,000 endowment given for the upkeep of the property.

The Church found a new role for itself, however, during the rise of the civil rights movement in the late 1950s and 1960s. The church has become an important center of civil rights activism and a pioneer in providing social services to its severely disadvantaged community and embracing the cause of African-American and women's rights. It was the site of nationally significant events, including the National Conference on Black Power (1968), the Black Panther Conference (1970), and the first ordination of women in the Episcopal Church (1974).

The church contains a collection of wall murals that are large and painted in the bright colors of the 1970s. They depict the "stations of the civil rights movement," a play on the traditional "stations of the cross." The murals provide a dramatic juxtaposition with the medieval style of the church and document the critical social role of inner-city churches.

It was designated a National Historic Landmark in 1996 for both its role in African American civil rights and its remarkable Gothic Revival architecture.

Cliveden (Chew House)

6401 Germantown Ave., Philadelphia; (215) 848-1777; cliveden .org; open Apr through Nov; admission charged

During most of the year, Benjamin Chew, chief justice of the Province of Pennsylvania, and his family lived in a townhouse in Philadelphia. He purchased Cliveden in Germantown, constructing the house from 1763 to 1767. Like many other wealthy Philadelphians, he built his country estate to remove his family from the threat of regular yellow fever epidemics during the summer months. Cliveden is an excellent example of late-Georgian architecture. The main house is two and a half stories high with a facade built of ashlar stone, and the other elevations stuccoed and grooved to simulate ashlar. The gable roof has arched dormers with flanking scrolls and a heavy cornice with modillions. Five large urns are positioned on the roof. The central door is pedimented with two flanking engaged Doric columns.

During the American Revolution, Chew first supported the colonial cause. As the conflict grew, his Quaker upbringing, close ties to the Penns, and unwillingness to support the revolution led to the loss of his government position. Along with Governor John Penn, he was held under arrest at Union Forge in New Jersey from 1777 to 1778.

In late September 1777, British soldiers occupied Philadelphia. The British army quartered several thousand troops in the village of Germantown, about 6 miles

northwest of the city near Cliveden. In October General George Washington was plotting to recapture Philadelphia from the northwest, straight through Germantown. Through the early morning hours of October 4, 1777, 12,000 men moved forward hoping to catch the British by surprise. However, the British were prepared, and the heavy fog caused confusion among the American troops. British troops barricaded themselves inside Cliveden, which proved to be an impenetrable fortress and this unexpected battle caused the Americans to miss their rendezvous with other segments of the army. The Americans lost the battle, but the combination of the strong effort at Germantown and a victory at Saratoga secured French support for the American cause, a turning point of the war.

Chew decided to maintain a low political profile for the remainder of the American Revolution. In the fall of 1779 he sold Cliveden and went into self-imposed exile with his family to his plantation near Dover, Delaware. In 1797 Chew repurchased Cliveden, and the Chews continued to occupy Cliveden for seven generations.

Cliveden was designated a National Historic Landmark in 1961. The Chew family donated Cliveden, including its remaining 5.5 acres, and their artifact collection to the National Trust for Historic Preservation in 1972. Over 230,000 documents were contained in the Chew family papers that documented the enslaved Africans and servants of the Chew family, not just at Cliveden but including their many plantations throughout Pennsylvania, Maryland, and Delaware. An in-depth study of these papers that began in 1994 has grown into a project that has re-written the history of Germantown. The Emancipating Cliveden project focuses on the exploration of slavery and its ongoing impact for all Americans, telling the whole story in ways that allow visitors to question their assumptions about American history by examining its many contradictions.

The College of Physicians of Philadelphia Building (The Mütter Museum)
19 S. 22nd St., Philadelphia; (215) 563-3737; collegeofphysicians .org; open year-round; admission charged

The College of Physicians of Philadelphia Building houses the headquarters, library, and museum of the oldest private medical society in the United States. Founded in 1787 as a membership organization of physicians, the College of Physicians has been distinguished for its contributions to medical research and education. With a goal to advance the science of medicine and reduce human suffering, 24 Philadelphia physicians founded this institution. Its membership has included some of the leading American physicians and surgeons of the last three centuries. Nearly 1,500 elected members (fellows) still meet at the college to work on the improvement of medical services to the public.

The College is the home to one of the finest museums of medical history, the Mütter Museum. In 1858 Philadelphia physician Thomas Mütter donated his personal collection of bones, plaster casts, medical illustrations, and other pathological artifacts to the College. His gift of specimens along with $30,000 was meant to create a museum for the purpose of medical research and education. As the museum grew and expanded, it forced the College to consider how to accommodate both the museum and its expanding library collection. It was decided that the College must build a new headquarters. Completed in 1909, the building is an excellent example of the Beaux Arts style, influenced by the classical design of the Royal College of Physicians in London built in 1673 to 1677. Its ornate architectural details of carved swags, panels, and scrolls convey the feeling of a private club, yet it houses a professional library and museum. It was designated a National Historic Landmark in 2008.

The Mütter Museum contains an unusual collection of anatomical specimens, models, and medical instruments displayed in cabinets. This type of cabinet museum was popular in the 19th century and has been preserved here. Some of the more unique items in the collection include the conjoined liver of "Siamese twins" Chang and Eng, the jaw tumor of President Grover Cleveland, and Einstein's brain. Despite its invitation to visitors to be "disturbingly informed," the museum helps the public understand the mysteries and beauty of the human body and appreciate the history of diagnosis and treatment of disease. While visitors focus on the unusual specimens in the museum, the College continually seeks to advance the cause of health and foster an ongoing exploration of the limitations and possibilities of the human body.

Conrad Weiser House
28 Weiser Ln., Wormelsdorf; (610) 589-2934;
conradweiserhomestead.org; house open Apr through Dec; grounds
open year-round; donations encouraged

Johann Conrad Weiser was born in Germany in 1696 and migrated to New York with his family in 1710. At the age of 16, with his father's permission, he went to live with the Iroquois. He became proficient with the Mohawk language and learned the customs of the Iroquois. He returned to his family in 1713.

In 1720 Weiser married Anna, and in 1729 they bought a farm in Berks County, Pennsylvania. They built a house of native limestone that was expanded several times over the years. It still retains an original single room with a fireplace and bake oven and a second room that Weiser added in 1750.

Weiser became friends with Shikellamy, an Oneida chief who was sent to Pennsylvania to manage relations with the British. Shikellamy trusted Weiser because of his time with the Iroquois in New York. Together they traveled to Philadelphia, where they met with the colony's chief justice, James Logan, to discuss ongoing relations between the Iroquois and the colonists. Logan relied on Weiser as an interpreter and negotiator with the Six Nations of the Iroquois. Weiser's knowledge was employed to negotiate a series of land ownership treaties between the Pennsylvania

colonists and the Iroquois. Weiser is credited with continuing the stable relationship between the Iroquois and the Pennsylvania colony during the 1730s and 1740s.

Weiser was appointed Lancaster County magistrate in 1741. He continued to serve as an interpreter and negotiate matters between the Iroquois and the colonies and traveled on behalf of the Pennsylvania government. When he visited New York in 1750, he discovered that while the Mohawk tribe remained loyal to the British, several of the other tribes of the Six Nations were developing stronger relations with the French.

By 1754 tensions were rising, and the British, with Weiser's help, hoped to gain the support of the Six Nations against the impending war with France. Unfortunately the Iroquois were no longer willing to offer support as a whole, and the Six Nations were acting independently. The Seven Years War (also known as the French and Indian War) began that same year. In 1755 the "Penn's Creek Massacre" resulted in the death of several colonists from Indian attacks. Weiser was asked to lead a local militia, and in 1756 he was named a lieutenant colonel in the Pennsylvania regiment; he was responsible for a line of forts between the Susquehanna and Delaware Rivers. In 1758 he negotiated the Treaty of Easton, the peace agreement to end the Seven Years War. Weiser died in 1760 at his farm in Wormelsdorf and is buried in the family cemetery.

The Conrad Weiser Homestead is a 26-acre site owned by the Commonwealth of Pennsylvania and managed by the Pennsylvania Historical and Museum Commission supported by the Friends of Conrad Weiser Homestead, a nonprofit group that is responsible for the day-to-day operation of the site. Three of the seven existing buildings are open to visitors. The site was designated a National Historic Landmark in 1960.

Cornwall Iron Furnace
94 Rexmont Rd., Cornwall; (717) 272-9711; cornwallironfurnace .org; open year-round Thurs through Sun; admission charged

Cornwall Iron Furnace is an intact example of the type of iron-making complex that manufactured most of America's iron from before the American Revolution until after the Civil War. The furnace, operated from 1742 to 1883, was a major producer of cast iron. It is probably the best-preserved charcoal furnace in the United States. The Cornwall Ore Banks, mined continuously from 1742 to 1973, were the largest known deposit of iron ore in the country until 1887.

In the 1730s Peter Grubb, a stone mason, began mining here. In 1742 he established the furnace. Grubb's father emigrated from Cornwall, England; he named the area Cornwall. The British Parliament tried to control the production of iron in America in 1750, but it had no effect and production increased. The American

colonies, with Pennsylvania being the top producer, smelted one-seventh of the world's iron at that time. In 1754, upon Peter's death, the land and business were inherited by his sons.

The Cornwall operations involved almost 10,000 acres and required miners, woodcutters, colliers, farmers, and servants. The most skilled laborers were those employed in the furnace. The furnace's primary product during the Grubb period was pig iron. Cornwall pig was processed in the forges on site and was also sold to local forges. Cornwall also manufactured cast-iron products, including stoves, and produced cannon and shot.

After the Revolutionary War, production at Cornwall Furnace was reduced. The Grubbs took on a non-family member, Robert Coleman, as a partner with a one-sixth share in the furnace, mines, and related properties. Coleman was enterprising, gaining full control of the operations by 1798 and eventually becoming one of Pennsylvania's first millionaires. The furnace continued to operate until changes in technology using anthracite coal-fired furnaces made the Cornwall operation obsolete. It closed in 1883.

The furnace was abandoned, leaving the building virtually untouched until it was given to the Commonwealth of Pennsylvania in 1932 by the Coleman family, along with an endowment for its maintenance. The ore mine continued to operate until 1973. The mine was purchased by Bethlehem Steel, and ore was extracted through both underground and strip-mining operations between 1917 and 1922. The open pit mine began to flood in 1972 and is now filled with water.

The Cornwall Iron Furnace grounds include the Ironmaster's mansion (now a private retirement center), charcoal barn (now the Visitor Center), the furnace building, and other buildings associated with the operation. Minersvillage (now private residences) is a collection of picturesque company-built stone houses. The historic site is administered by the Pennsylvania Historical and Museum Commission. It was designated a National Historic Landmark in 1966. It has also been designated a National Historical Landmark by the American Society of Metals, and a National Historic Mechanical Engineering Landmark by the American Society of Mechanical Engineers.

Eastern State Penitentiary
2027 Fairmount Ave., Philadelphia; (215) 236-3300; easternstate .org; open year-round; admission charged

The Eastern State Penitentiary, built to apply the Pennsylvania system of imprisonment, served as a model for prisons throughout the world. This system, developed by the Philadelphia Society for Alleviating the Miseries of Public Prisons, founded in 1787, was grounded in the Quaker concept of reflection in solitude. It took almost 20 years before the Pennsylvania legislature appropriated $100,000 for the erection of a prison based on the system of solitary confinement. A design competition was held, and John Haviland, already a successful architect, won the commission in 1822. Haviland's design reflected the commission's requirement that "the exterior of a solitary prison should exhibit as much as possible great strength and convey to the mind a cheerless blank indicative of the misery that awaits the unhappy being who enters within its walls."

Haviland designed a building with seven cellblocks radiating out of a central rotunda, all enclosed by massive stone walls resembling medieval battlements. Each cell was self-contained with its own ventilation and lighting and an exercise yard so that prisoners would have no contact with each other. The first prisoner was admitted in 1829. Delegations came to Philadelphia to study the Pennsylvania System and its architecture. And the architectural masterpiece drew many tourists to Philadelphia during the 1830s and 1840s as well. But this system of solitary confinement

was controversial, and many people debated whether it was inhumane to withhold visitors and all contact with family. With no contact from the outside world, people wondered, was this type of confinement even effective? The debate continued for many years, and in 1913 the Pennsylvania system was abolished.

The prison remained in use and was enlarged many times, hosting a few infamous inmates. Alphonse "Scarface" Capone, arrested for carrying a concealed weapon, spent eight months here in 1929 to 1930. It was his first prison sentence. Capone's cell on the Park Avenue Block was almost luxurious including furniture, oriental rugs, and a radio. William Francis "Slick Willie" Sutton, one of the most famous bank robbers in America, spent 11 years here. In 1845 he was one of eleven prisoners who escaped through an inmate-dug tunnel that extended 100 feet. Sutton was recaptured a few minutes later, the first of the escapees who all were eventually returned to prison. During his time here, Sutton made five escape attempts.

By the 1960s the prison needed costly repairs butit continued to operate. The Commonwealth closed the facility in 1971. The City of Philadelphia purchased the site in 1980 hoping to reuse or develop it. The penitentiary was opened for guided tours in 1994 by the Pennsylvania Prison Society. In 1997 the Society signed a 20-year agreement with the City to continue to operate the site.

The Eastern State Penitentiary Historic Site, Inc., was formed as a nonprofit organization in 2001 and continued the agreement with the City to keep the historic site open. They have transformed a collapsing, once-dangerous property into a thriving cultural attraction that hosts 250,000 visitors each year. The organization has continued to restore and preserve the site and have carefully interpreted the complex story. Their work has earned many awards for high-quality restoration and interpretation. The site was designated a National Historic Landmark in 1965.

Edgar Allan Poe House
532 N. Seventh St., Philadelphia; (215) 965-230; nps.gov/edal; open year-round; no admission charged

While Philadelphia was the home of writer Edgar Allan Poe for only six years (1838 to 1844), he was at his happiest and most productive here. He worked as an editor for one of the nation's most popular magazines, *Graham's Lady's and Gentleman's Magazine*, and a few of his most famous stories were written here, including the "Fall of the House of Usher," "The Murders in the Rue Morgue," and "The Mask of the Red Death." Poe, his wife Virginia, and his aunt Maria Clemm moved to this red brick house in 1843. It was in this house that he wrote the short stories "The Tell-Tale Heart" and "The Black Cat." The latter includes a description of a basement very similar to the basement in this house. "The Black Cat" was published in the *Saturday Evening Post* on August 19, 1843.

Edgar Poe was born in 1809. When his mother died of tuberculosis in 1811, Edgar was taken in by merchant John Allan and his wife. They raised Edgar, giving him his middle name, but never legally adopting him. He entered the University of Virginia in 1826. He excelled at his studies but could not complete them because Allan refused to pay Edgar's debts, a large portion incurred from gambling. Unable to support himself, Poe enlisted as a private in the US Army in 1827. Eventually earning the rank of sergeant major, he left military service and hired a substitute to complete his obligation.

A brief reconciliation between Poe and Allan occurred upon the death of his stepmother in 1829. Because Poe was will facing his earlier desertion from the Army, Allan helped him receive an honorable discharge and secure an appointment to West Point Military Academy. Entering West Point in 1830, Poe realized that literature was his true calling. He longed to leave West Point but Allan refused to help him again. Poe worked to accumulate demerits and offenses until he was ultimately court-martialed and was expelled.

Poe moved to Baltimore, where he lived with his impoverished aunt and her daughter Virginia. Poe continued to write and had literary success as an editor. In 1836 he married Virginia, his 13-year-old cousin. After an unsuccessful move to New York, the Poes and Mrs. Clemm moved to Philadelphia in 1838. Virginia contracted tuberculosis in 1842. Her illness and their constant financial problems

caused Poe to sink into deep bouts of depression. In 1844 Poe left Philadelphia for New York, with his ailing wife and aunt and only $4.50 in his pocket. Virginia died in 1847. He died two years later at the age of 40.

Edgar Allan Poe's writings have been described as horrifying and brilliant, but he continually struggled with mental illness and debt. Of all the places Poe lived while in Philadelphia, this is the only one that remains. The Edgar Allan Poe House is owned by the National Park Service and is operated as a historic site. It was designated a National Historic Landmark in 1962. Annually the Poe House, in partnership with the German Society, hosts the Poe Arts Festival, a celebration of the life and work of the writer.

Elfreth's Alley
124–126 Elfreth's Alley; Philadelphia; (215) 574-0560; elfrethsalley .org; exterior accessible year-round; guided tours and museum open weekends in season or by appointment; admission charged

This block-long alley was opened in 1706 by the mutual agreement of two adjoining landowners who combined their properties between Front Street and Second Street to open a cart path to the river. It now survives as the oldest unchanged and continuously inhabited street in Philadelphia. Thirty-two narrow two- and three-story houses built between 1720 and 1830 line the alley, their facades flush on the narrow sidewalks. Primarily occupied by artisans and tradesmen, the houses are a rare intact

collection of 18th- and early-19th-century housing stock. The alley was not referred to as Elfreth's Alley until 1750. It was named for Jeremiah Elfreth, a blacksmith who lived on Second Street, just north of the alley. He acquired title to both sides of the alley and built and rented out many of the homes. Eighteenth-century Philadelphia was in an economic boom. Most of the houses in Center City were home to prosperous businessmen and speculators. This created a demand for artisans who could produce the goods and services a growing city needs. Cabinetmakers, silversmiths, glass blowers, and wagon builders occupied Elfreth's Alley, and they were able to serve the demand for their wares.

The Elfreth's Alley Association was established in 1934 to safeguard the unique character of this charming street. In 1966 they had the street designated a National Historic Landmark to ensure that the construction of Interstate 95 did not destroy the colonial history. The Elfreth's Alley museum preserves the 18th-century home of a pair of dressmakers. Restored to a Colonial-era appearance, exhibits in the house and tour guides interpret the life of the houses and alley's residents in that era. Bladen's Court, located midway down the street, is an alley within an alley that leads to a charming circular courtyard.

The Alley is still a thriving residential community that is home to artists, educators, and entrepreneurs. Two annual events offer the only opportunities to tour the interiors of these private homes. Fete Day in June and Deck the Alley in December are festivals that highlight the importance of the oldest continuously inhabited street in the United States.

Ephrata Cloister
632 W. Main St., Ephrata; (717) 733-6600; ephratacloister.org; open year-round; admission charged

The buildings of the Ephrata Cloister, built between 1740 and 1746, are some of the best examples of authentic Germanic/Medieval architecture in Pennsylvania. This very early collection of buildings with their steep, expansive gabled roofs and long, shed-roofed dormers reflects the traditional craftsmanship of Germany brought to America.

The Cloister was founded in 1732 by Conrad Beissel, a German Pietist who came to the site seeking to live as a hermit following his own religious ideas. He lived his life on Earth preparing for the Second Coming and his spiritual meeting with God that he believed would occur very soon. In 1735 he organized the Society of the Solitary, one of the earliest religious and communal sects in the United States practicing mystic religious observances, celibacy, and social and economic activities.

Ephrata is known as the birthplace of American Fraktur (a highly artistic writing style). The Ephrata drawings utilized pale colors and soft tones rather than the much

brighter colors of later Pennsylvania Germans who followed in their path. Fraktur seems to have been used first to illustrate the 1746 Ephrata community song book with the title, *The bitter good, or the song of the lonesome turtledove, the Christian church here on earth, in the valley of sadness, where it bemoans its widowhood and at the same time sings of another, future reunion,* a collection of hundreds of hymns composed by Conrad Beissel and his followers.

By the early 1750s, nearly 80 celibate Brothers and Sisters were housed in the Germanic log, stone, and half-timbered buildings. Wearing white robes, they adopted sparse diets and lived a life of work and silent prayer as they prepared for their heavenly existence after the Second Coming. Nearly 200 family members (known as householders) lived in homes and farms nearby. During the American Revolution, members nursed 500 wounded soldiers from the Battle of Brandywine at the Cloister.

The three main buildings of the Cloister were the Saal (Chapel) built in 1740, the Saron (Sisters' House) built in 1742, and the Bethania (Brothers' House) built in 1746. The Bethania was demolished in 1920, but the two earliest buildings remain along with a bake house, several cabins and cottages, and the Academy, built in 1837.

The community declined after the death of Beissel in 1768, and by 1800 most of the celibate members had died. In 1814 the remaining householders incorporated the Seventh Day German Baptist Church and remained there until the church closed in 1934.

In 1941 the Commonwealth of Pennsylvania acquired the site. The Pennsylvania Historical and Museum Commission is responsible for the administration of the Cloister and for operating a program of research, restoration, and interpretation with the support of the Ephrata Cloister Associates. The site was designated a National Historic Landmark in 1967.

Fairmount Water Works
660 Waterworks Dr., Philadelphia; (215) 685-0723; fairmountwaterworks.org; open year-round Tues through Sun; no admission charged, donations welcome

Following a series of yellow fever epidemics in the late 18th century (which at the time was thought to be caused by unclean water), city leaders appointed a "Watering Committee" to propose a solution. Benjamin Latrobe designed the first water system in 1799 in Centre Square, which used two steam engines to pump water from the Schuylkill River into wooden tanks. The two 57,000-gallon tanks used gravity to direct the water into wooden water mains. The system did not work well, and if one or both steam engines stopped working, the water stopped flowing. A new system would be needed to meet the demand.

Construction of the Fairmount Water Works was started in 1812, and the system was in operation in 1815. Designed by Frederick Graff (an apprentice of Latrobe), the water works at Fairmount was opened as a steam pumping station with two steam engines. The machinery was housed in a group of four Greek Revival buildings situated on a terrace above the Schuylkill River. The grounds were landscaped and became a central focus of Fairmount Park, one of the first parks in the

United States. The mechanics of the operations were considered an engineering success, and the classically inspired architecture of the buildings became a popular tourist destination.

Water was drawn from the Schuylkill River and pumped uphill 96 feet to the reservoir located at the top and water was gravity-fed to homes and pumps. The high expense of operation, estimated at $30,858 annually for either engine, and the need for a greater supply of water, led the city to consider alternative systems in 1819. The City purchased the water power rights of the Falls of the Schuylkill and between 1819 and 1821, a dam was constructed to create a pond. A water power system, employing paddle wheels, pumped the water to the reservoir. This was the first use of paddle wheels for this purpose in the United States.

Keeping up with changing technology, the paddle wheels were replaced by turbines in 1867, also a first in the United States. With continual changes in technology, the existing water works became obsolete and were closed in 1911. The arches in the forebay of the building were filled in and the building was converted into the Philadelphia Aquarium. The reservoirs were drained, and construction of the Philadelphia Museum of Art began in 1919 on the reservoir site.

Through a concerted effort of public and private agencies since 1974, Fairmount Water Works has been restored and reused. Owned by the City of Philadelphia Water Department, it is operated by the Fairmount Water Works as an educational facility and event center. The Fairmount Water Works was designated a National Historic Landmark in 1976. It is also a Civil Engineering Landmark and a National Mechanical Engineering Landmark.

First Bank of the United States
116 S. Third St., Philadelphia; (215) 965-2305; nps.gov/inde; not open to the public, but part of the National Park Service's Independence National Historical Park

The United States, after its newly won freedom, was dealing with massive debt and an uncertain future. Secretary of the Treasury Alexander Hamilton had the idea to establish a national bank. The idea sparked rage and heated debate among early leaders. Thomas Jefferson, in particular, was a strong and vocal opponent and urged President Washington to veto the bill after the Senate and the House approved it in February 1791. Washington gave Hamilton one week to address Jefferson's concerns, and Hamilton delivered a 15,000-word rebuttal that swayed Washington.

The Bank of the United States, now known as the First Bank, received a 20-year charter from Congress in 1791. It was the closest thing to a national currency at a time when each state could print its own banknotes. Only First Bank notes were

accepted to pay federal taxes, and, in turn, the First Bank was responsible for paying the government's bills including the debt left from the Revolutionary War.

The First Bank was initially housed in Carpenters' Hall (see related entry) but moved into its new home in 1797. Samuel Blodgett Jr., architect and "Superintendent of Buildings" for the new capital in Washington, D.C., designed the building in 1794. The building was considered an architectural masterpiece. The bank is a three-story brick building with a blue marble facade. Its seven-bay front, with a large Corinthian-columned portico, is the work of Claudius F. LeGrand and Sons, stone workers, woodcarvers, and guilders. The tympanum, a decoration within the flat area of the triangular pediment, contains elaborate mahogany carvings of a fierce-eyed eagle grasping a shield of 13 stripes and stars and standing on a globe festooned with an olive branch. The hipped roof is covered in copper. The building is a notable early example of the Classical Revival style.

Congress opted not to renew the bank's charter when it expired in 1811. Stephen Girard purchased most of its stock, the building, and furnishings and opened his own bank. Girard's bank was the principal source of credit during the War of 1812, placing most of his resources at the disposal of the US government. The bank also underwrote 95 percent of the war loan. Girard Bank eventually built a new building and vacated this space. In 1955 the National Park Service acquired the building and uses it for park offices. It was designated a National Historic Landmark in 1987. Although it is closed to the public, it is a popular photo spot within Independence National Historical Park.

Fonthill Castle
525 E. Court St., Doylestown; (215) 348-6098; mercermuseum.org/
visit/fonthill-castle

Mercer Museum
84 S. Pine St., Doylestown; (215) 345-0210; mercermuseum.org

Moravian Pottery and Tile Works
130 E. Swamp Rd., Doylestown; (215) 348-6098; buckscounty.org/
mptw

All sites open year-round; admission charged

Henry Chapman Mercer, antiquarian, proponent of the Arts and Crafts Movement, and visionary designer planned and built three buildings in Doylestown, designated collectively as a National Historic Landmark in 1985.

Mercer planned his residence from the interior out; he did not consider the exterior at all until the rooms were designed. In 1907 he began by imagining each of the rooms. He made clay blocks to represent the rooms and stacked them on top of each other, rearranging them until he had a general outline of the building. He created a plaster model as a reference and began construction. Fonthill was loosely based

on medieval castles that Mercer had seen in his travels. He was one of the pioneers in the use of reinforced concrete as a building material because it was durable, fire-proof, and pliable when poured. The concrete was mixed by hand, formed, and then embellished with red tile. The plan of the house is irregular in shape and height, including a four-story tower and steeply pitched hip, gable, and pyramidal roofs. The house was completed in 1912. Fonthill also includes a cast-concrete garage with a large second-story balcony and chimney pots that are dove cotes, a spring house decorated with tiles, and concrete entrance gates.

The Moravian Pottery and Tile Works is a U-shaped building constructed around an open courtyard. Built in 1911 and 1912, it is two and a half stories in height, built of reinforced concrete with concrete buttresses, resembling a medieval cloister. The roof is a concave hip covered in tiles, irregular chimneys, and windows. A variety of decorative tiles are set in both the interior and exterior walls. Concrete barrel-vaulted interiors house five pottery kilns. It is a working museum that still functions as a manufacturer of architectural tiles produced in a manner like that developed by Mercer himself. Mercer tiles have been used extensively across the United States, including an impressive installation in the Pennsylvania State Capitol in Harrisburg (see related entry).

There were no plans or drawings for the 1916 Mercer Museum; workmen just followed the direction of Henry Mercer. The museum, much larger than his house, is also built of reinforced concrete and resembles Fonthill with towers, chimney dove cotes, and turrets. It is 115 feet high and contains 297 windows. The interior is open from floor to ceiling with a ramp that begins at ground level and leads to a balcony that runs continuously past 40 alcoves filled with the tools of 40 crafts and trades. It is the most comprehensive museum collection of its type in the world.

When Henry Mercer died in 1930, he left Fonthill in trust as a museum of decorative tiles and prints and gave life tenancy to his housekeeper. In 1990 the Bucks County Historical Society was appointed the permanent trustee. Fonthill and the Mercer Museum are operated by the Bucks County Historical Society. The Moravian Pottery and Tile Works is operated by the Bucks County Department of Parks and Recreation.

Fort Mifflin
Fort Mifflin & Hog Island Rds., Philadelphia; (215) 685-4166; fortmifflin.us; open Mar 1 through Dec 15, Wed through Sun; admission charged

This star fort on Mud Island in the Delaware River was built in 1772 by the British to defend the water approach to Philadelphia. Fort Mifflin has a long history of military use and is now operated as a historic site. The physical layout and architecture of the site reflect the period 1777 to 1875, but military interpretation highlights the Fort's service during each of America's major wars: the Revolutionary War, the

War of 1812, the Civil War, World War I, and World War II. It was designated a National Historic Landmark in 1970.

When the British captured Philadelphia in September 1777, General Howe, commander of the British forces, needed to get supplies to his troops. A fleet of British ships was south of Philadelphia in the Delaware Bay. Howe gave the order to sail up river. The Americans had secured the British-built Fort Mifflin, just below the city, and had 400 men garrisoned there. They were charged with holding off the British so that Washington and his exhausted army could move into winter quarters at Valley Forge. For nearly six weeks, American forces in Fort Mifflin and Fort Mercer, in New Jersey, kept the British ships from making it to Philadelphia.

Early in the morning on November 10, 1777, the British ships launched a full canon assault on Fort Mifflin. The bombardment continued for days, with the Americans working at night to repair the day's damage. Finally, on November 15, the two main supply ships sailed to Philadelphia, protected by 182 cannons against Fort Mifflin's 10. Exhausted, cold, and out of ammunition, the men at Fort Mifflin evacuated to Fort Mercer, setting fire to the fort before they left. Fort Mifflin, rebuilt during John Adams's administration, was occupied by the Americans in the War of 1812.

Repairs to the fort, completed in 1863, returned Fort Mifflin to active service as a military prison. Prisoner exchanges were a common occurrence early in the Civil War. But when the Confedercy refused to exchange black Union soldiers in 1862, the practice stopped. This created an overpopulation of existing prisoner-of-war camps, and both sides had to find places to serve as prisons. To handle the large influx, many buildings, including tobacco warehouses, civilian prisons, and coastal forts such as Fort Mifflin, Fort McHenry in Baltimore, and Governors Island in New York, were converted to hold military prisoners. Fort Mifflin held three kinds of prisoners: Confederate prisoners of war, Union soldiers, and civilians. In July 1863 Fort Mifflin began receiving Confederate prisoners of war captured during the Battle of Gettysburg (July 1 to 3, 1863).

During the First and Second World Wars, Fort Mifflin was part of the US Navy Ammunition Depot. Fort Mifflin was decommissioned by the federal government in 1954, after 183 years of service. The Commonwealth of Pennsylvania acquired the property and transferred ownership to the City of Philadelphia in 1962. The nonprofit, Fort Mifflin on the Delaware, was founded to manage and interpret the site in 1986.

Friends Hospital

4641 Roosevelt Blvd., Philadelphia; (215) 831-4600; friendshospital .com; exterior accessible year-round

Friends Hospital opened in 1813 as the first private nonprofit hospital in the United States devoted exclusively to treating mentally ill patients. Originally known as the *Friends Asylum for the Relief of Persons Deprived of the Use of Their Reason*, it is the oldest continuously operating mental hospital in the United States. The social and medical concerns that Quakers held regarding psychiatric problems guided Friends Hospital in its physical site plan and methodology of treatment. These approaches, then novel, became the model studied throughout the 19th and early 20th centuries.

The "moral treatment" that was advocated by Quakers was a radical departure from the common practices toward the mentally ill. The Quakers would not employ the usual practice of confinement; physical restraint, sometimes with chains; severe physical punishment; and allowing the visiting public to stare and laugh at the patients. The main purpose of "moral treatment" was to strengthen the mental wellness of each patient, and they concentrated on strengthening mental *health*, not on curing mental *illness*. This was a departure from the accepted practice, and the guiding principle on which all the hospital's procedures were based. The policies of the Friends Asylum were to provide supportive, nurturing, and clean surroundings with privacy from the public; excellent living conditions with plenty of healthy food; vigilant attention from the staff and visitors; physical exercise and recreation; learning

opportunities; and creative outlets such as needlework or art. Patients participated in on-site horticulture programs that included cultivating the hospital's food crops, creating scenic walks and outdoor plantings, working in the greenhouses to supply indoor plants and floral arrangements, and using the grounds for recreation.

The hospital continued to be a leader in the care of mental health patients. As early as 1830 a pet therapy program was introduced. By the 1850s the Quaker approach to mental health had become the example for America. In 1889 they were among the first to accept women psychiatric physicians when Anna Broomall, M.D., joined the staff. That same year they opened the nation's first institutional gymnasium. In 1894 one of the first two-year training schools for nurses who wished to specialize in mental health was introduced. It was unique in including certifications in both general and psychiatric nursing. In 1896 they graduated their first class of two men and four women.

Friends Hospital still welcomes patients to a quiet refuge to begin a healing process on its large campus in Northwest Philadelphia. Much of its 100 acres remains as lawns, gardens, stream valley, and forest. The site was designated a National Historic Landmark in 1999.

Fulton Opera House
12 N. Prince St., Lancaster; (717) 394-7133; thefulton.org; theater open year-round, purchase tickets through the box office; tours offered on Fri during the summer; admission charged

In 1852 Christopher Hager, a civic leader in Lancaster, hired architect Samuel Sloan to design a building that could be used for a community center. The building was constructed on the foundation of Lancaster's first jail. It was named Fulton Hall, after Lancaster native Robert Fulton, who is credited with inventing the first commercially successful steamboat in 1807. In 1854 Hager commissioned a statue of Fulton that was placed in a third-story niche above the entrance. The hall was used for meetings, lectures, concerts, and theatrical performances.

In 1856 the hall was sold to Blasius Yecker, who undertook a major renovation following the Civil War. Architect Edwin Forrest Durang lowered the auditorium, added space for stage rigging, constructed a proscenium arch, and added the first balcony. The name was changed to Yecker's Fulton Opera House and the grand opening on October 2, 1873, was a performance of *Othello*, benefiting widows and orphans of the Civil War.

Yecker's son Charles assumed management of the Fulton in 1903. He commissioned C. Emlen Urban, a local and highly respected architect, to redesign the interior. The performance space was again enlarged, and eight box seats, the grand staircase, and foyers were added. The second balcony or "Peanut Gallery" was added and furnished with wooden benches. The "Peanut Gallery" offered the cheapest

seats and often the rowdiest crowd, who would throw peanuts at the performers if they didn't enjoy the show. The Fulton hosted many popular performers, including Sarah Bernhardt and George M. Cohen. It even hosted a production of *Ben Hur* that included a live chariot race on stage. After 1910, movies pulled audiences away from live theater, and with fewer traveling shows available, Yecker started his own theater company. To meet the changing tastes of audiences, the Fulton offered burlesque shows beginning in the 1920s, which resulted in a local group, the Law and Order Society, to have Yecker arrested for his immoral shows. Yecker sold the building, and the new owner continued to produce a few stage shows and began showing movies.

A fundraising campaign began in the early 1950s to restore the theater and to begin producing local productions and hosting touring companies. A "grand reopening" celebration was organized to honor the Fulton's 100th anniversary. Despite efforts surrounding the 100th anniversary, business was poor. In October 1957 the Fulton reopened as the Fulton Art Theatre and a new movie screen was installed.

The Fulton Opera House was saved from the wrecking ball in 1962 by a local group that included Nathaniel E. Hager, great-grandson of the original founder of the Fulton. They raised the funds to purchase the building and formed a non-profit, the Fulton Opera House Foundation. Starting in 1989 the Fulton launched a campaign to raise funds to restore the theater to its original Victorian elegance and update the facilities. Completed work was celebrated with a gala in 1995.

Since 1852 the Fulton Opera House has remained open—making it one of the oldest continuously operating theater buildings in the nation. The Fulton Theatre, the current name of the facility, produces seven full productions and four family shows each season. It was designated a National Historic Landmark in 1964.

Furness Library, School of Fine Arts, University of Pennsylvania
229 S. 34th St., Philadelphia; (215) 898-8325; library.upenn.edu/ finearts; open weekdays, year-round; no admission charged

Frank Furness, a Philadelphia native, is recognized as one of the most important architects of the 19th century. The cornerstone of his library at the University of Pennsylvania was laid in 1888, and the building was completed in 1890. The overall appearance of the stone-trimmed red brick structure has an ecclesiastical appearance, with both Romanesque and Gothic elements, including gargoyles and distinctive, monumental foliate (leaf) carvings. The entrance is a massive porch of dressed stone that leads into the entry that is dominated by a great iron staircase that rises the full height of the 95-foot tower. Considered innovative at the time, it was the first library to separate the reading room and book stacks. Books were kept in a separate room that was designed so the rear wall could be removed on jackscrews and new bays added as needed. Light flows through translucent glass floors and a sloping glass

roof. Beautiful leaded-glass windows are embellished with quotes from Shakespeare and Greek and Latin classics. The quotes were chosen by Horace Howard Furness (Frank's older brother), a Shakespearean scholar and prominent member of Penn's faculty in the late 19th century.

Frank Furness was born in Philadelphia in 1839. He was educated at private schools in the city, but never attended a college or university. In 1857 he became an apprentice to architect John Fraser. Two years later he entered the New York studio of Richard Morris Hunt, where he learned the eclectic medieval form that became his signature style. Furness served in the Union cavalry for most of the Civil War. At the conclusion of the war, he returned to work for Hunt.

Upon returning to Philadelphia, Furness entered into his first architectural partnership in 1867, shortly thereafter known as the firm of Furness and Hewitt. During the early 1870s this team designed the Pennsylvania Academy of Fine Arts, the commission that established Furness as one of the major artists of his generation. Hewitt left the firm in 1875, and Furness worked alone until 1881, when he made his chief draftsman, Allen Evans, a partner in the firm of Furness and Evans. By the time of his 50th birthday in 1889, Furness had designed more than 300 buildings in Philadelphia, including several major city landmarks. The Pennsylvania Institute of Architects was formed in 1869, with Furness as one of the cofounders.

The Furness Library was the first library on the Penn campus. Though it was designed to accommodate decades of collection expansion, the building was overcrowded by the first decade of the 20th century. Over the next 30 years, several major alterations and additions were made to accommodate heavier-than-expected use and to house various special collections. The Furness Library was designated a National Historic Landmark in 1985. A major restoration was completed in 1990. In 1992 the building and library were renamed the Anne and Jerome Fisher Fine Arts Library to honor the principal donors to the restoration project.

George Nakashima Woodworker Complex

1847 Aquetong Rd., New Hope; (215) 862-2272; nakashimawood workers.com; tours offered first Sat (Apr through Oct); donations requested

The George Nakashima Complex is a historic artists' compound consisting of houses and studio buildings designed and built by artist George Nakashima (1905–1990) that served as a family home and studio space. It was designated a National Historic Landmark in 2014.

George Nakashima was born in 1905 in Washington State. His extensive education included the study of forestry and architecture while attending the University of Washington, L'Ecole Americaine des Beaux Arts in Paris, Harvard, and the Massachusetts Institute of Technology, graduating with a master's degree in architecture in 1930. Returning to Paris to work with architect Antonin Raymond, a Czech

American, they traveled to Tokyo to collaborate with Frank Lloyd Wright, who was designing the Imperial Hotel. Nakashima learned traditional building techniques and designs while in Japan and met Marion Okajima.

Nakashima and Okajima returned to the United States and married in 1941. Disenchanted with the practice of architecture, Nakashima became interested in furniture making. When the Japanese attacked Pearl Harbor in 1941, anyone of Japanese ancestry living on the West Coast was forced into internment camps. The Nakashimas, including their newborn daughter Mira, were relocated to Idaho. In 1943 he asked his former employer, Raymond, to petition for his release. Since some of Raymond's jobs were US government–related, Nakashima could not work as an architect. Instead Raymond hired him to work on his New Hope farm.

In addition to his farm duties, Nakashima set up a small workshop and began his career in furniture making. In 1946 he approached a nearby farmer and asked him if he could have three acres of land in exchange for doing carpentry work. The farmer agreed and Nakashima constructed his workshop, while he and his family lived in a tent. As the furniture business grew, so did the complex of buildings. In 1956 Nakashima began using experimental roof designs, particularly the conoidal shell (cone shape) and hyperbolic paraboloid (saddle-shaped curve), for buildings on the property. In addition to designing, Nakashima took a hands-on approach to the construction. He was his own general contractor on each project, directing the work and performing some of the work himself.

The complex grew to 12 acres and includes 18 buildings, a mix of residential and business use. All the buildings are designed in the International Style, infused with Japanese elements. The main building is the Conoid Studio, built in 1960, with a concrete roof in the shape of a sine wave. The walls are a mix of stone, concrete, cement blocks, and glass. Nakashima's involvement in the furniture business continued until his death in 1990. His designs are known for using wood in as close to its natural state as possible, often retaining the free edge of the tree to keep a natural shape. The business continues under the direction of his daughter Mira. The eight studio-related buildings are open to the public. The Nakashima Foundation for Peace oversees the complex with a mission to maintain the architecture and furniture Nakashima designed and built on this property.

Graeme Park
859 County Line Rd., Horsham; (215) 343-0965; graemepark.org; open year-round, Fri through Sun; admission charged

Provincial Governor of Pennsylvania Sir William Keith constructed this house between 1721 and 1722. The property was originally called Fountain Low because of the many natural springs surrounding the home. Keith used the 1,700-acre

property as a summer residence, including the stone house, a long-house for servants, a barn, and a malt house. The relatively plain two-and-one-half-story house is built of brown fieldstone with tall narrow windows and doors, topped by a high gambrel roof. A conflict with the Penn family caused Keith to be removed as provincial governor. He traveled back to England in hopes of a new appointment but died before he could return to his family.

In 1739 Fountain Low was purchased by Dr. Thomas Graeme, husband of the governor's stepdaughter. Renaming it Graeme Park, he transformed it into an elegant residence for summer entertaining, which reflected his social prominence. Realizing that little could be done to modify the mansion's stone exterior, Graeme extensively remodeled the interior to reflect the Georgian style and taste of the mid-1700s. Elaborate paneling was installed in several rooms, and fine marble and imported ceramic delft tiles surround the fireplaces. Upon his death in 1772, the property was inherited by his only surviving child, Elizabeth. Unlike most women of her day, Elizabeth was exceptionally well educated and is credited with hosting America's first salons or literary gatherings. She was also a woman whose life was marred by tragedy and controversy. After a failed relationship with Benjamin Franklin's son William, she married Henry Hugh Fergusson, a poor Scottish immigrant. During the American Revolution, Fergusson declared loyalty to Great Britain. He left for England after the withdrawal of the British, never returning to his wife in America. His loyalty to Great Britain resulted in the Colonial government seizing Graeme Park in 1778, and most of the contents were sold. Elizabeth was eventually able to regain control of the property in 1781.

After Elizabeth's death in 1801, the main section of the property that included the house was sold to the Penrose family. They occupied the existing house until their new home was built on the grounds. The museum's visitor center is located in a bank barn that was also constructed by the Penrose family. Welsh Strawbridge, who bought the property in 1920, continued to maintain the original stone house although they did not live in it. In 1958 the Strawbridges gave the land and buildings to the Commonwealth of Pennsylvania. Although the original acreage has been reduced to 42 acres, the house, barn, and land retain the feel of an early country estate. Graeme Park is operated by the Pennsylvania Historical and Museum Commission and supported by the Friends of Graeme Park. It was designated a National Historic Landmark in 1960.

Grey Towers
450 S. Easton Rd., Glenside; (215) 572-2900; arcadia.edu/story/ story-grey-towers-castle; open year-round; tours can be arranged through the Society for Castle Restoration at Arcadia University (SCR@arcadia.edu)

In 1893 William Welsh Harrison, the 31-year-old co-owner of the Franklin Sugar Refinery, hired 25-year-old architect Horace Trumbauer to design a new home. The architect planned for a three-story grand structure with 41 rooms, inspired by Alnwick Castle in England. The stone for Grey Towers Castle was quarried in nearby Chestnut Hill, and Indiana limestone was crafted into exterior trim for doors, windows, and other elements. Local craftsmen were employed for the vast amount of hand-carved woodwork for the interior. The main rooms of the house are decorated in French styles that extend from the Renaissance to the era of Louis XV.

At age 16, after dropping out of school, Horace Trumbauer apprenticed himself to George and William Hewitt, a firm that excelled in English design and gave a young Louis Sullivan, the father of the modern skyscraper, his first job. After an almost six-year apprenticeship, Trumbauer formed his own firm at age 21 and

quickly made an impression designing modest residential commissions. He was paid $171 with a $7 stipend for transportation for his first job. Grey Towers was Trumbauer's first major project and launched a career that included commissions from many wealthy Philadelphians. Other large residences soon followed, including Chelton House (1896) and Lynnewood Hall (1898), both in Elkins Park. Ties to wealthy clients in Philadelphia led to commissions in Newport, Rhode Island, and across the country, including town houses in New York, Philadelphia, and Washington. He designed several hotels, office buildings, medical school buildings, and private clubs in Philadelphia. He also designed campus buildings for Harvard and Duke Universities. Trumbauer does not have the name recognition of many of his turn-of-the-20th-century peers. He was very private and avoided interviews. His work, however, is well-known and admired in the Philadelphia area. During his career Trumbauer's work evolved with changing styles from French Classical to Art Deco, helping his firm maintain a full schedule of work through the Depression. He passed away in 1938.

Beaver College (now Arcadia University) purchased Grey Towers in 1929, two years after Harrison's death. At the time, Beaver College was in Jenkintown and held classes both there and in Glenside at Grey Towers. In 1962 the college moved permanently to the Grey Towers property. The building was designated a National Historic Landmark in 1985.

The castle now houses the administrative office. The third floor offers traditional dorms and suites to select freshmen. Downstairs, the Rose and Mirror Rooms frequently hold lectures, book readings, and panel discussions.

Gruber Wagon Works
1102 Red Bridge Rd., Reading; (215) 249-0100; co.berks.pa.us/ Dept/Parks/Pages/GruberWagonWorks.aspx; open year-round; admission charged

When constructed by Franklin H. Gruber in 1882, the Gruber Wagon Works was situated in Pleasant Valley on Licking Creek, a tributary of Tulpehocken Creek. The family-owned Gruber Wagon Works produced both standard farm wagons and custom vehicles from 1882 to the 1950s. Until the automobile came into general use in the early 20th century, America depended on wagons, carriages, and horse carts for most of their transportation. The Gruber family stopped manufacturing wagons in the 1950s but continued to make wagon repairs in the factory until 1972. The wagon works, with all its original tools and machinery intact, is a unique example of an early and important 19th-century American industry.

The wagon works is a two-and-one-half-story, cross-shaped, gable-roofed frame structure that consisted originally of a single rectangular main block and a small ell. In 1905 and 1906 the Grubers added a second ell to the northwest (front) of the building to house a hand-operated elevator and a painting and drying division. The shop evolved from a single craftsman shop using hand tools into a business that employed up to 20 men using mass-production methods. The process did not

include an assembly line. Rather, the parts were transported back and forth between the various rooms. The bench shop constructed the wagon wheels, and the wood shop used patterns to produce the wooden parts of the wagon. Tires were mounted to the wheels, and the blacksmith shop added the iron components and assembled the wagons. The paint shop added distinctive striping and scrollwork by hand. Most of the tools were belt-drive from an overhead drive system powered by a 1906 Otto gasoline engine.

In the 1970s, the US Army Corps of Engineer's Blue Marsh Lake flood-control project included the impounding of Tulpehocken Creek and flooding 2,200 acres, including the site of the wagon works. The Moss-Bennett Act (originally the Reservoir Salvage Act) made it possible to use federal funds to safeguard the historic site. In 1976 and 1977 the wagon works was dismantled and moved 5 miles east. The new location resembles the old one, near the north bank of the Tulpehocken Creek. Moving a historic site from its original location can negatively affect its historic designation on the National Register of Historic Places. The care that was taken in documenting, dismantling, and reassembling the wagon works allowed its historic designation to remain in place.

The building has been carefully restored and is now a museum. It is owned by Berks County and is located at the Berks County Heritage Center. It was designated a National Historic Landmark in 1978.

Harrisburg Station and Train Shed
Fourth & Chestnut Sts., Harrisburg; (800) 872-7245; amtrak.com/ stations/har; open year-round; no admission charged

The Pennsylvania Railroad (PRR) was chartered in 1846 to construct a line between Harrisburg, the state capital, and Pittsburgh, the gateway to the West. This line was meant to improve upon the Pennsylvania Main Line Canal route that relied on a series of inclined planes to transfer canal boats up and over the Allegheny Mountains (see related entry on Allegheny Portage Railroad). The PRR line to Pittsburgh was completed in 1855, and the PRR grew into the largest and most important railroad in the United States.

The Harrisburg Station is the third station built on this location by the PRR. It was constructed between 1885 and 1887, at a time when Harrisburg was a major railroad center. The first-floor interior originally contained a gentlemen's waiting room, a ladies' waiting room, a restaurant, and a ticket office. The first major alteration occurred in 1902 with the addition of a three-bay, two-story baggage room; a new passenger tunnel between the station and shed; and overhead passenger bridges. In 1904 the station was severely damaged by fire and was completely remodeled.

More significant than the station are the two train sheds located to the rear of the station. The shed nearest the station was built in 1885; the second shed was built sometime after 1896. Both train sheds are constructed of structural steel columns with timber and steel trusses spaced 20 feet apart. Albert Fink, engineer for the Baltimore & Ohio Railroad, patented the prototype for a truss in 1854 that was a significant innovation in American civil engineering. In addition to being used in roof construction, as in this instance, Fink trusses were also effective for long-span bridges.

By the 1960s competition from private automobiles, buses, and airplanes caused a sharp decline in train travel. The PRR merged with its longtime rival, the New York Central, creating the Penn Central Railroad in 1968. Just two years later, the Penn Central was bankrupt. With railroad passenger service struggling throughout the country, the federal government created the National Railroad Passenger Corporation, better known as Amtrak, in 1971 to consolidate and operate the nation's long-distance passenger trains.

By this time the Harrisburg station, along with many other formerly grand stations, was in poor condition. In 1974 Harrisburg City Council, Amtrak, and others were dedicated to rehabilitating the station for multimodal use. In 1976 the Harrisburg Train Station, including its train sheds, was designated a National Historic Landmark and Amtrak leased the station and train sheds to the Harrisburg Redevelopment Authority for a 30-year period to access funding streams that made the restoration possible. It was rehabilitated for modern use while carefully preserving its most important features. Now the Harrisburg Transportation Center, the lower

level serves as a terminal for Greyhound and Trailways buses, several local commuter buses stop at the station, and Amtrak operates a line that serves Philadelphia and Pittsburgh with daily commuters and travelers.

Hill–Physick–Keith House
321 S. Fourth St., Philadelphia; (215) 925-7866; philalandmarks .org/physick-house; open year-round; tours available, schedule varies; admission charged

Philip Syng Physick was born July 7, 1768 in Philadelphia. Philip enjoyed working with his hands and wanted to join his grandfather as a goldsmith. His father wanted him to study medicine. After graduating from the University of Pennsylvania with an art degree, he began the study of medicine with a local physician. In 1788 Physick studied in London with Dr. John Hunter, the leading anatomist and surgeon of the period. He spent a year working with Dr. Hunter at London's St. George Hospital and then went to Edinburgh, where he graduated with his degree in medicine in 1792.

Physick entered private practice when he returned to Philadelphia. He befriended Dr. Benjamin Rush, eminent physician, writer, educator, and a signer of the Declaration of Independence whose connections helped Physick's practice flourish. Physick became the physician of Stephen Girard, philanthropist and banker who would personally save the US government from financial collapse during the War of 1812. Physick was elected to the staff of the Pennsylvania Hospital (see related entry) in

1794 at age 26. He also conducted classes at the University of Pennsylvania, where a special chair of surgery was created for him in 1805. Physick suffered many illnesses throughout his life. As a child he had small pox, and during both yellow fever epidemics of 1793 and 1798, he contracted the disease while working long hours in the local hospitals. In 1813 he had another attack of fever, probably typhoid, from which he never fully recovered. In 1819 the University of Pennsylvania suggested that he take over as chair of anatomy, resigning his position as chair of surgery. Although Physick continued to practice medicine, his activities declined markedly after 1820.

This house was built in 1786 for Henry Hill, a wealthy Philadelphia importer. Hill occupied the house until his death in 1790. After Hill's death Miss Abigail Physick purchased the property for her brother, Philip. It is the only free-standing Federal townhouse remaining in Society Hill. With its huge fan light over the door and the grand proportions and straight, classical lines, Physick House is an exceptional example of the Federal style. The first floor of the house includes an entry with a marble tiled floor, three parlors, and two kitchens. The main rooms have stucco cornices, marble trim, and two carved marble mantelpieces. The second floor has six rooms and five marble mantelpieces. The third floor has five rooms and four marble mantelpieces. The house is furnished with French-influenced Neoclassic wallcoverings, draperies, and furnishings of the period.

Physick lived in the house until his death in 1837. It remained in the family until 1965, when it was sold to the Annenberg Fund, which presented it to the Philadelphia Society for the Preservation of Landmarks. Since 1930 the Society has restored, furnished, and operated several house museums in Philadelphia, including the Hill-Physick-Keith House. The house was designated a National Historic Landmark in 1976.

James Buchanan House (Wheatland)
230 N. President Ave., Lancaster; (717) 392-4633; lancasterhistory .org; open year-round; admission charged

James Buchanan, 15th president of the United States, purchased this large Federal-style house and its 22 acres of land near Lancaster in 1848. Buchanan was born in 1791 in Mercersburg, Franklin County. He was educated at Dickinson College in Carlisle, Cumberland County. He moved to Lancaster to study law, and he passed the bar and remained in Lancaster for the remainder of his life. He served in the military during the War of 1812 and was a member of the Pennsylvania legislature for two years.

Elected five times to the US House of Representatives, Buchanan was a gifted debater and well versed in the law. Buchanan made three unsuccessful bids for the presidency, but his reputation as a compromiser made him an acceptable Democratic candidate in 1856. Wheatland became the symbol of his "front porch" campaign, a low-key campaign where candidates remain close to home.

As tensions over slavery escalated between the North and South, voters elected Buchanan as president in 1856 in the hope he could achieve a peaceful settlement of

the issue. As the only unmarried president, Buchanan had his niece, Harriet Rebecca Lane Johnston, act as First Lady of the United States. The Dred Scott decision that gave slaveholders the right to transport human property freely, blocked anyone of African descent from becoming a citizen, and declared that Congress did not have the power to regulate slavery was announced two days after he took office in 1857. By 1858 the government was almost unable to function. The Northern-controlled House had their legislation blocked by strong Southern votes in the Senate, and tensions between the North and South were almost to the breaking point.

Buchanan had pledged that he would not seek a second term, so the presidential election of 1860 pitted two Democratic candidates (North and South), a Constitutional Union Party candidate, and Abraham Lincoln, representing the Republican Party, against each other. Lincoln won despite his name not even appearing on any ballots in the South. Outraged by the results of the election, South Carolina seceded from the Union, and six other states followed. James Buchanan returned to Wheatland in March 1861, unable to affect any change in the tensions between the states during his presidency. The country was about to engage in war. Buchanan died at Wheatland in 1868.

Built in 1828, Wheatland was constructed with a brick two-and-one-half-story central section flanked by three-story wings. The interior has a central hall with two matching rooms on each side. Buchanan made very few changes to the house, and it retains its elegant Federal-style appearance.

The George B. Willson family, the last private owners of the house, bequeathed half of the property to the Lancaster County Historical Society. Recognizing its importance, the Junior League of Lancaster raised funds to purchase the remainder of the property in 1936. They began work on its preservation and eventually transferred the entire property to the historical society. It was designated a National Historic Landmark in 1961. The house is furnished with period pieces and many of the items belonged to Buchanan, particularly those in the library. Wheatland is owned and operated by LancasterHistory.org.

John Bartram House
5400 Lindbergh Blvd., Philadelphia; (215) 729-5281; bartramsgarden.org; grounds open year-round, no admission; tours available weekends Apr through Dec, admission charged

John Bartram (1699–1777), a third-generation Pennsylvania Quaker, was a self-taught collector of plants. He was considered the first American botanist of note, and through his extensive correspondence and travels, he brought native plants to the attention of botanists around the world. In 1765 he was appointed botanist to

King George III. On his field trips, he recorded not only botanical specimens, but everything he observed: wildlife, the people, and the earth itself.

John Bartram purchased 102 acres in west Philadelphia along the Schuylkill River in 1728. He began construction of his house in 1730, incorporating the existing structure into his design. He enlarged the house as the family grew, even lifting the peak of the roof in 1770 and extending the house toward the river. The interior of the house is characterized by its woodwork, paneled walls, many closets, and deep window sills. The layout of the house includes a door to the outside from almost every first-floor room. The stone outbuildings, all built by the Bartrams, include the seed house (1737), the stable and carriage shed (1743), and the barn (1775).

His garden was a source of pleasure for luminaries like Thomas Jefferson and George Washington who visited him often. It was also the heart of his livelihood. Philadelphians regularly came to purchase seeds and plants for cooking and medicinal use. As early as the 1750s, lists of his offerings appeared in London publications. Three generations of Bartrams continued operation of the international plant and nursery business after his death.

The Bartram garden extends from the house to the river. William Bartram (1739–1823) continued his father's exploration of native American plants. John Bartram Jr.'s daughter, Ann Bartram Carr (1779–1823), was educated by her uncle William and had the skill to illustrate the plants they grew. Ann and her husband, Colonel Robert Carr (1778–1866), continued to operate the international seed and plant business. The gardens were maintained from John Bartram's time up to 1850, when they were abandoned. A campaign to preserve Bartram's Garden began

after they were threatened by development resulting in the City of Philadelphia taking ownership in 1891. Descendants of John Bartram created the John Bartram Association in 1893. In 1923 active restoration was begun. Eighty-two varieties of plants were recorded at that time down from 129 varieties, 70 years earlier. A careful replanting of the garden is restricted to only plants grown there by John and William Bartram.

Bartram's Garden is a 45-acre National Historic Landmark, designated in 1960, operated by the John Bartram Association in cooperation with Philadelphia Parks and Recreation.

John Wanamaker Store
1300 Market St.; Philadelphia; (215) 241-9000; visitmacysusa.com/ Philadelphia; open year-round; no admission charged

John Wanamaker, a native Philadelphian born in 1838, is credited with developing the first department store, and his innovative practices set the standard for the future of retailing. In 1861 Wanamaker and his brother-in-law, Nathan Brown, opened Oak Hall, a men's clothing store. As early as 1870 the Oak Hall store had annual sales of over $2 million and an excellent reputation. Wanamaker is credited with introducing the price tag. Purchases prior to that were accomplished with haggling. He thought everyone should receive an equal price.

Wanting to expand, he purchased a Pennsylvania Railroad depot and in 1876 opened Wanamaker's Grand Depot. In 1878 Wanamaker became the first to install lights in his show windows, which led to the fashionable practice of "night window shopping." In 1880 Wanamaker was the first store to install Edison's new incandescent lamps. After only three years of operation, the store had expanded to 49 departments. Catering to an upscale market, he promised quality goods with a money back guarantee. The first copyrighted store advertisement was printed in 1874. He claimed that his advertisements were truthful and that he would stand behind them. When the public learned that he was sincere, business boomed and he earned the trust of his customers.

Building on his success, Wanamaker built a 12-floor building in three stages between 1904 and 1910 on the site of the Grand Depot. He built in stages to allow the Grand Depot to continue operating. The new building was designed by Daniel H. Burnham, an architect credited with helping shape the department store. Burnham gained fame as one of the leaders of the 1893 World's Columbian Exposition in Chicago that launched the City Beautiful Movement and brought classically inspired architecture back to popularity. Designed in the Renaissance Revival style, Wanamaker's is a steel-framed, granite-faced building with an elegant interior. The new store contained nearly 45 acres of floor area, 10 floors of merchandise, the largest dining room in Philadelphia (the Crystal Tea Room), 2 auditoriums (Greek Hall and Egyptian Hall), and the Grand Court, the symbolic heart of the building. In 1911 President Howard Taft dedicated the department store, the only sitting president to ever do so.

The Grand Court features the iconic Wanamaker Organ, originally displayed at the St. Louis World's Fair of 1904, purchased by Wanamaker and installed in the Grand Court in 1911. Thirteen freight cars transported the organ from St. Louis. Despite its size, the tone was judged inadequate to fill the huge court. Wanamaker opened a private pipe-organ factory in the store attic, employing up to 40 full-time employees to enlarge the instrument. He increased the number of pipes, first by 8,000 between 1911 and 1917. Then, between 1924 and 1930, he added 10,000 more pipes, which brought the total to 28,500. Free organ recitals have been offered daily since 1911.

The Wanamaker Eagle, also purchased at the St. Louis World's Fair, is a 10-foot, 2,500-pound bronze sculpture made by German sculptor August Gaul. Generations later, locals still ask friends to "meet at the Eagle" in the Grand Court.

In 2006 the building was purchased by Macy's, Inc., and continues to operate. The building was designated a National Historic Landmark in 1978.

Johnson House

6306 Germantown Ave., Philadelphia; (215) 438-1908; johnsonhouse.org; open Sat year-round, other times by appointment or by season; admission charged

The Johnson House was built from 1765 to 1768 by John Johnson Sr., as a wedding gift for his son John Johnson Jr., a tanner and farmer who operated the tannery business from his home. The Johnson House is believed to be the oldest residence built for year-round living still standing in Germantown. From 1770 to 1908 the Johnson House functioned as a residence for five generations of the Johnson Family. It is significant for its role in the antislavery movement and the Underground Railroad. The Johnson House was a key site in Philadelphia during the 19th-century movement to abolish slavery in America. The house was the family home of Rowland Johnson (1816–1886), a Progressive Quaker who achieved national prominence as a vice president of the American Anti-Slavery Society. Working closely with black and white abolitionists and assisting fugitive slaves and freedmen on their journeys to freedom, members of the Johnson family were among the leading abolitionists of their generation.

The Johnson House is a rectangular five-bay, two-and-a-half-story Georgian stone residence. The main house is essentially as it was when erected in the 1760s. It retains nearly all its original 18th-century features intact, both exterior and interior. The house stood vacant from 1908 to 1917, when it was sold to the Woman's Club of Germantown for use as a club house. For more than 50 years the house was the meeting place and social center for hundreds of clubwomen. However, by the 1970s membership in the club had declined, and title was transferred to the

Germantown Mennonite Historic Trust, Inc., on the condition that the Johnson House be maintained as a museum open to the public. The house was designated a National Historic Landmark in 1997. The ownership was transferred to the Johnson House Historic Site, Inc., in 2002. Since that time the nonprofit organization has undertaken a multiyear plan to preserve and restore the building.

Keim Homestead
99 Boyer Rd., Oley; (610) 385-4762; historicpreservationtrust .org/historic-properties/jacob-keim-farmstead; open year-round by appointment only; no admission charged

The Keim Homestead is an exceptionally significant example of vernacular architectural traditions from German-speaking Europeans on the architectural landscape of America during the mid-18th century. German-American colonists were living in large concentrations between New York and Georgia at the time, and their influence on social, cultural, and economic life has greatly influenced American history. The Keim House and the ancillary house are showpieces of early German-American domestic architecture and tradition.

The house was built for Jacob and Magdalena Keim around 1753 and was inhabited by their descendants until 1911. The two-and-one-half-story limestone structure is an example of the *Flurküchenhaus* (entry-kitchen) house type, the most

common Germanic house plan during the time. It is comprised of three rooms grouped around a massive internal chimney sited off-center. The three rooms are the *Küche*, or kitchen; the *Stube*, or stove room; and the *Kammer*, or chamber. The central chimney was a key element of the type, since its location was necessary for the placement of a stove, which heated all three rooms. The exterior foundation and walls are limestone, and the roof was originally red clay tile. All the exterior openings have segmented arches. A northern block was added as the family grew, although the only interior access to this addition is through the attic.

Located adjacent to the main house is a rubble stone ancillary house. This structure also dates to 1753 and is Germanic style. The building has a vaulted root cellar for the storage of vegetables and is built into a bank. There is a spring flowing through the cellar. The portion of the basement that was used as a dairy was whitewashed. The window and door openings have segmented arches like those on the main house. The ancillary house has a central chimney and a tile roof.

There is evidence that the ancillary building was a turner's shop. Jacob Keim was a turner, a woodworking artisan who turned spindle-form pieces such as railing balusters and furniture legs on a lathe. Evidence remains of the place where the pole lathe was attached at the ceiling, and racks that held chair parts remain. There is a depression in the floor made by the use of a foot treadle. To the left of the lathe is a large iron door that opens into the flue of the fireplace below; workers could open the door and sweep shavings into this fireplace. An

enclosed chamber adjoining the chimney stack originally provided an excellent place to dry wood before turning. The large window in the gable end was for back-lighting the lathe, which is helpful when turning wood. The big window around the corner would have provided additional light to the work area.

The Keim Homestead was designated a National Historic Landmark in 2016 and is owned by the Historic Preservation Trust of Berks County. The Trust owns and maintains eight historically significant buildings in Berks County.

Laurel Hill Cemetery
3822 Ridge Ave., Philadelphia; (215) 228-8200; thelaurelhillcemetery.org; open year-round; no admission charged

Designed by Scottish architect John Notman in 1836, Philadelphia's Laurel Hill Cemetery was his first known commission, launching his career as a nationally renowned architect and landscape gardener. John Jay Smith established this large, rural (at the time) cemetery outside Philadelphia. He felt it was his civic duty to develop a cemetery that would accommodate the increasingly large population of Philadelphia. At a time when American cities suffered from crowding, disease, and scarcity of public space, cemeteries like Laurel Hill offered a reprieve. Originally 32 acres Laurel Hill was situated on top of a hill overlooking the Schuylkill River. Its

romantic landscape, beautiful monuments, and impressive architecture made it a popular tourist attraction for picnics, carriage rides, and sightseeing.

Laurel Hill was expanded to 78 acres through the combination of four land parcels between 1836 and 1861. A system of winding roads and paths provides access to the cemetery's 51 sections, guiding visitors past hundreds of mausoleums and monuments. These vary greatly in size and style, displaying Roman and Egyptian iconography, Victorian opulence and eclecticism, and the early 20th century's taste for Art Nouveau and revivalism. On Ridge Avenue, a classically inspired gatehouse, built in 1836, marks the main entrance. The structure roughly resembles a Roman triumphal arch and unifies two separate living quarters, the Gardener's Lodge and the Porter's Lodge. The passageway that divides these spaces is covered by a coffered vault resting on colonnades. Upon entering the cemetery, a sculpture grouping is situated under a turreted enclosure. It consists of three sandstone figures carved in the mid-1830s by Scottish Sculptor James Thorn. Seated on a sarcophagus at the center of the composition is Thorn's representation of Old Mortality, an itinerant peasant who repairs the worn carvings of the dead on their tombstones in the fictional works of Sir Walter Scott. A statue of Scott himself gazes at the peasant, while Old Mortality's pony stands in the background.

Philadelphia's elite bought lots in the cemetery and commissioned monuments from the city's best-known architects and sculptors. The cemetery's most interesting and elaborate monuments are often biographical in design. The sarcophagus of industrialist Thomas Sparks shows his shot tower in low relief, while the tomb of Joseph Lewis depicts the Philadelphia Waterworks he helped establish. Following her death in Egypt, Mary Cooke was interred beneath a sarcophagus adorned with an illustration of the pyramids at Giza. Many prominent Philadelphians are buried here, including Harry Kalas, legendary sportscaster of the Philadelphia Phillies. Laurel Hill is also the final resting place of General George Gordon Meade, 39 other Civil War–era generals, and 6 *Titanic* passengers.

Laurel Hill Cemetery, still in active use as a burial ground, is supported by The Friends of Laurel Hill Cemetery, a nonprofit organization that preserves and promotes the historic character of Laurel Hill, undertaking restoration projects and offering educational programs, events, and tours. In 1998 Laurel Hill Cemetery was designated a National Historic Landmark, one of only a few cemeteries in the United States to earn that distinction.

Lightfoot Mill (The Mill at Anselma)
1730 Conestoga Rd., Chester Springs; (610) 827-1906; anselmamill .org; tours available weekends Apr through Dec, or by appointment; admission charged

Chester County's fertile soils were perfect for the growing of wheat, and the fast-running streams provided water power to grind the grain into flour. Samuel Lightfoot harnessed the water power on his land to build a custom gristmill around 1747. These small "custom mills," ground grain for individuals on a percentage basis, the miller typically collecting 10 to 20 percent as payment. The difficulties and high cost of transporting wheat and corn encouraged the construction of numerous custom mills that served a community within a radius of about 10 miles, the distance that a farmer could conveniently travel round-trip in one day. Gristmills were found in virtually all southeastern Pennsylvania townships after 1700. By 1781 Chester County had 127 mills.

Chester County had a growing livestock and dairy economy by the mid-19th century, and Lightfoot's Mill was an important part of that industry. The Pickering Valley Railroad connected the Anselma farmers in Chester County to the growing markets in Philadelphia by 1872.

The mill's final operator, Oliver E. Collins, and his family came to Anselma in 1919. When grain-milling technology changed, Collins installed machinery without destroying the Colonial-era power train system or the 1820s upgrades. Surviving the Great Depression, the Collins family used their gristmill to make a living by running a saw mill and a cider press in addition to continuing the milling of animal feed and grain. Collins served as the postmaster, operated a repair and sharpening service, and even cut hair.

The Lightfoot Mill continued operations for three centuries, serving the Anselma community and evolving to meet the needs as they changed. The Lightfoot Mill is likely the only surviving gristmill with an intact Colonial-era power transmission system in the United States. The mill retains much of its Colonial and 19th-century character. The second-floor offices of Collins and most of the machinery he used remains intact.

In 1983 the mill property was purchased by the French & Pickering Creek Conservation Trust from the estate of Oliver E. Collins. In 1999 the Mill at Anselma Preservation and Educational Trust was formed to complete the mill's restoration and operate the historic site. Tours and milling demonstrations connect visitors with the agricultural past. The mill sells its own stoneground flour and cornmeal and hosts a weekly farmers' market on its historic grounds. It was designated a National Historic Landmark in 2005.

Memorial Hall
4231 Avenue of the Republic, Philadelphia; (215) 581-3181; pleasetouchmuseum.org; open year-round; admission charged

Memorial Hall is the only major building remaining of the 200 that were constructed specifically for the 1876 Philadelphia Centennial Exposition, the first official World's Fair in the United States. It was held in Philadelphia to celebrate the 100th anniversary of the signing of the Declaration of Independence. The Centennial Exposition was attended by almost 10 million visitors from around the world. Thirty-seven countries provided exhibits.

Memorial Hall was designed by 30-year-old Herman Joseph Schwartzmann in a Beaux Arts style. The symmetrical facade with center and corner pavilions, triple arched entry portals, coupled columns, niches, and statues served as the exposition's art gallery. Schwartzmann also planned the exposition's grounds and 33 other fair buildings. After the exposition, Memorial Hall housed the Pennsylvania Museum of Industrial Art (now the Philadelphia Museum of Art.) The original collection included objects of an industrial nature, as well as fine and decorative art objects such as European ceramics. In 1928 the Museum of Art's new building opened with a record attendance of 1 million visitors in its first year. Memorial Hall continued to house the less important collections and was eventually turned back to the Fairmount Park Commission in 1954. The commission used it for its offices with a police station in the hall and a gymnasium and swimming pool in its wings. It was designated a National Historic Landmark in 1976.

By 2000 the building was in poor condition suffering from lack of maintenance and used only for the storage of art. Seeking a new location, the Please Touch Museum signed an 80-year lease for the building in 2005 and began an $85 million renovation to convert it into a children's museum. The museum opened its doors to the public in 2008. The Please Touch Museum was founded in 1976 and had several locations before selecting Memorial Hall for its permanent home. The building is filled with interactive exhibits where everyone is invited to play. It is also home to the Woodside Park Dentzel Carousel, built in 1908. After more than 40 years in storage at the Smithsonian and 2 years of restoration, the carousel is again operating with its horses, cats, rabbits, pigs, and goats at the Please Touch Museum.

Merchants' Exchange Building
143 S. Third St., Philadelphia; (215) 965-2305; nps.gov/inde/learn/ historyculture/places-merchantsexchange.htm; open year-round; no admission charged

Early in the nation's history, Philadelphia was a vibrant center of prosperity with an active commercial and financial district. For many years meetings between the Philadelphia merchants took place in small coffeehouses near the Delaware River waterfront. It soon became clear that a central location was needed for business transactions and negotiations. The importance of an exchange building was well established throughout the world, and several American cities were building exchange buildings in the late 18th and early 19th centuries. In 1831 a group of Philadelphia

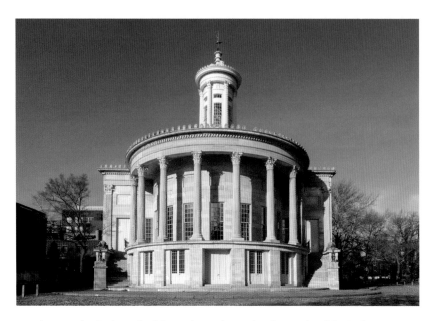

merchants, who had profited from the explosive local growth of the Jacksonian era, formed the Philadelphia Exchange Company and constructed a building to house this activity.

A call for designs for the new Philadelphia Exchange Company building yielded nine submissions, with the winning design being submitted by William Strickland. Strickland began his career as an apprentice at the age of 14 in the practice of Benjamin Henry Latrobe. By the time of his design submission for the Philadelphia Exchange Building, he was already enjoying great popularity as an architect, having completed the Second Bank of the United States (see related entry) and the Steeple at Independence Hall, and would become known as one of the leading American architects.

The Merchants' Exchange Building, originally the Philadelphia Exchange, was built between 1832 and 1834. Built on a triangular lot near the Delaware River and its related commerce to the east and the financial center of the city to the west, the monumental building is designed in the Greek Revival style with an overall rectangular shape, a semicircular extension with a two-story Corinthian portico, and a wealth of Greek Revival details. Following the War of 1812, Americans were increasingly rejecting British influence including the Georgian and Federal styles of architecture. As they looked to the ideals of Greek democracy as a model for the new nation, the classical orders of Greece also influenced architecture. By the 1830s the Greek Revival style was emerging as the model for modern American architects. For a time Greek Revival was considered the national style. Temple-fronted facades were common on churches, town halls, banks, and private houses.

Upon its completion, the Merchants' Exchange Building quickly became the financial center for Philadelphia with commercial enterprises, marine insurance companies, the Philadelphia Board of Trade, and the Philadelphia Stock Exchange located there. The US Post Office occupied a large room and was the first in the country to sell stamps.

Now part of Independence National Historical Park, the building serves as the park's headquarters. It was designated a National Historic Landmark in 2001.

Milton S. Hershey Mansion
100 Mansion Rd. E., Hershey; (717) 520-1100; hersheytrust.com; exterior accessible year-round; no admission charged

The name Hershey is synonymous with chocolate. But Milton S. Hershey (1857–1945) was not an immediate success in the business that made his Hershey Bar a generic term in America. As a teenager he apprenticed with a candy maker and found his life's work. However, his first and second candy businesses in Philadelphia and New York failed and bankrupted him before he was 30. Refusing to give up and using a skill he had learned in Denver for making caramels from fresh cream, he founded the Lancaster Caramel Company in 1891. With 1,400 employees he was shipping caramels all over the United States and Europe.

While attending the Columbia World Exposition in Chicago in 1893, Hershey was intrigued by an exhibit of German chocolate-making equipment. He purchased two machines and began producing chocolate coatings for his caramels. With the

demand for chocolate growing rapidly, he incorporated the Lancaster Caramel Company in 1894 and formed the Hershey Chocolate Company as a subsidiary. He retooled his operations and using a unique recipe for milk chocolate began mass-producing the chocolate bar. In 1900 he sold the caramel business to the American Caramel Company but kept the Hershey Chocolate Company.

In 1903 Hershey built a factory in Derry Township, Dauphin County, exclusively devoted to producing a good-quality chocolate product that was affordable to all. He also believed that workers who were treated fairly would be better workers. He established a company town, eventually known as Hershey, which included housing, schools, churches, public transportation, recreation, and cultural opportunities. In 1907 he opened a park that expanded rapidly to include amusement rides, a swimming pool, and a ballroom. Trolley cars and trains brought thousands of out-of-town visitors to enjoy Hershey Park. In 1971 it was redeveloped as Hersheypark, one of America's most popular theme parks.

Hershey and his wife Catherine built a home, known as Highpoint, on Chocolate Avenue in 1908. Designed by well-known Lancaster architect C. Emlen Urban, it is a two-and-one-half-story Colonial Revival limestone house with a two-story flat-roofed portico supported by Ionic columns. It is situated on a slight rise that allowed Hershey to see the original factory to the west. Unable to have children, the Hersheys founded a school for orphaned boys in 1909. In 1918, after the death of his wife, he endowed the Milton Hershey School with his entire fortune of Hershey Chocolate Company stock.

In 1930 Hershey donated Highpoint to a newly formed country club, reserving only a small second-floor apartment for himself. He lived there until his death in 1945. The house is situated in the middle of the Hershey Country Club. In 1977 the Hershey Company purchased the house for its corporate headquarters. It was designated a National Historic Landmark in 1983. It houses the offices of the Hershey Trust Company, a real estate management firm that manages the Milton Hershey School Trust, the M. S. Hershey Foundation Trust, and the Hershey Cemetery Trust.

Mother Bethel A.M.E. Church
419 Sixth St., Philadelphia; (215) 925-0616; facebook.com/ MotherBethel; tours available Tues through Sat, and after service on Sun; no admission charged

In 1760 Richard Allen was born into slavery to Benjamin Chew, a wealthy landowner and chief justice of the Supreme Court of Pennsylvania. Chew owned numerous properties, including Cliveden in Germantown (see related entry). Allen's family was purchased by a Delaware planter when he was 7 years old. Later his mother

was sold along with three of his siblings. The three remaining siblings, including Richard, remained in Delaware. Allowed to attend church by his owner, Allen joined the Methodist faith. When his owner also joined the Methodist faith, he arranged for Allen and his brothers to buy their freedom, believing that he could not get to heaven owning slaves.

Allen, no longer a slave, followed his calling and began preaching throughout Delaware, New Jersey, and Pennsylvania. In 1786 the Methodist elders called him to Philadelphia to minister to the blacks of the congregation at St. George's Methodist Episcopal Church. Black participation in church services was tolerated if they occupied the "Negro pews" and otherwise kept their place. However, as Allen's preaching attracted more black parishioners, white hostilities increased. As tensions escalated, so did the realization that a separate church was needed. Allen founded the Bethel African Methodist Episcopal Church in 1794. Originally in a frame building on the same site as the present church, Mother Bethel is a memorial to Richard and his work founding the A.M.E. denomination. Mother Bethel refers to this as being the original church of this denomination.

Allen wanted a church that would speak to the political, social, and economic needs of his congregation. His church provided services that were not extended to blacks by the white municipal government. Allen and Bethel Church fought the Black Codes that would have prohibited blacks entering the free states of the North. Allen opposed the black laws being passed in Northern states and worked for the advancement of free blacks and the abolition of slavery. He died in 1831.

The present church, fourth on the site, is a monumental granite-faced building dating from 1889. It is Romanesque Revival in style with a square tower and a large circular entrance. Circular stained-glass windows were made in Heidelberg, Germany. A basement crypt houses Richard Allen's tomb and a museum that contains Allen's bible and pulpit. The building was designated a National Historic Landmark in 1974.

Mount Pleasant
3800 Mt. Pleasant Dr., Philadelphia; (215) 763-8100; parkcharms .com/mount-pleasant; open daily, Apr thorough Dec; admission charged

Mount Pleasant, located in Fairmount Park on the east bank of the Schuylkill River, has been called the most important Georgian house in this region. Built in 1761 and 1762 by John Macpherson, Scottish sea captain and privateer, the mansion is probably the only regional surviving example of a symmetrical late-Georgian composition of three units, found so frequently in the South. The exterior is rubble masonry coated with stucco, scored to resemble stone masonry, with prominent brick quoins

at the corners. The east and west facades are identical, with pavilions framing arched doorways, with Palladian windows above, opening onto each end of the second-floor hall. It is also one of the finest and most elaborate examples of a late Georgian interior in the United States.

Builder-architect Thomas Nevell, an apprentice to Edmund Woolery, the builder of Independence Hall, designed and built Mount Pleasant, a country estate and farm. Macpherson and Nevell shared the goal of making this house remarkable and notable. Macpherson desired to be accepted into Philadelphia society and wanted a house that would be compared favorably to the best of the city homes. Nevell wanted to showcase his talent as a builder and architect. Mount Pleasant was one of the most elaborate homes along the Schuylkill River. John Adams visited in 1775 and proclaimed it "the most elegant seat in Pennsylvania."

After suffering financial setbacks, Macpherson leased Mount Pleasant to the Spanish ambassador at the start of the American Revolution. In 1779 he sold the property to General Benedict Arnold, who was in command in Philadelphia following the evacuation by the British, although he never lived there. After passing through several owners, it was purchased in 1792 by General Jonathan Williams, the first superintendent of West Point and grand-nephew of Benjamin Franklin. He lived there intermittently for 20 years. His children sold the estate to Fairmount Park in 1868.

Prior to its restoration in 1926 by the Philadelphia Museum of Art, it was used commercially as a beer garden and a dairy farm. Mount Pleasant is administered by the Philadelphia Museum of Art, owned by the City of Philadelphia, and operated as a house museum. It was designated a National Historic Landmark in 1974.

N. C. Wyeth House and Studio
13 Murphy Rd., Chadds Ford; (610) 388-2700; brandywine.org;
access only via shuttle from the Brandywine River Museum of Art (1
Hoffman's Mill Rd., Chadds Ford); guided tours Apr through Nov;
admission charged

The Newell Convers Wyeth House and Studio sits on an 18-acre property just east of the Brandywine Creek. The buildings and idyllic setting have strongly influenced the life and career of one of the most successful illustrators of all time. Despite national recognition for his easel paintings (he was elected to the National Academy in 1941) and for public and private mural commissions, N. C. Wyeth (1882–1945) was best known for his illustrations in books and magazines. Like Wyeth, many other great painters worked as illustrators, including Winslow Homer and Frederick Remington. Wyeth's best paintings are the subjects he knew best, the rural farm scenes that surrounded his home and anchored his life.

During the early decades of this century, when Americans relied on books and periodicals for information and entertainment, Wyeth created illustrations that excited the imagination of generations of readers. In a career that spanned four and a half decades, Wyeth illustrated some 90 books, including *Treasure Island*, and countless stories for such prestigious magazines as *Harpers* and the *Saturday Evening Post*. Book jackets that included the line "Illustrated by N. C. Wyeth" often shared equal space with authors such as Robert Louis Stevenson and Arthur Conan Doyle.

The N.C. Wyeth House, built in 1911, was designed in the Colonial Revival style. The main feature on the front facade of the house is the balcony, running the length of the main section and supported by five square wooden posts and a cross-hatch railing pattern. There is a large, gabled wall dormer in the center. The Wyeth Studio, also built in 1911, is a four-part, one-story building that is composed of three studios, one included originally, a mural studio added in 1923, and a studio for Wyeth's daughter Carolyn added in 1931.

Wyeth's son Andrew (see related entry) was already a well-known painter when Wyeth died tragically in a railroad crossing accident in 1945. Wyeth's wife and daughter continued to live on the property, making no major changes in the house or studio. Mrs. Wyeth died in 1973. Carolyn Wyeth, who inherited the property from her mother, taught art classes in the studio in the 1950s and 1960s. Through the generosity of the Wyeth family, the ownership of the property passed to the Brandywine Conservancy in 1982. Carolyn Wyeth continued to live on the property until her death in 1994. The property is operated by the Brandywine River Museum of Art. It was designated a National Historic Landmark in 1997. Visitors to the N. C. Wyeth House and Studio can see the studio much the way it looked in 1945, showcasing the life and personality of the artist.

New Century Guild
**1307 Locust St., Philadelphia; (215) 735-7593; newcenturytrust
.org; exterior accessible year-round**

The New Century Guild of Working Women, established in 1882, was founded by
Eliza Sproat Turner, a writer who led the Women's Congress and the *New Century
for Women* newspaper at the Philadelphia Centennial Exposition of 1876. She was
socially active in the antislavery and women's suffragette movements. Initially a committee of the New Century Club, the guild was dedicated to helping "self-supporting
women" at a time when many believed that no self-respecting woman would work
for pay outside her home.

The Guild offered vocational training, classes, and social opportunities for working women. The classes and programs offered by the guild increased, and as demand
grew for these programs, the group needed to secure its own building. In 1893 the
guild's leadership created the New Century Trust and began raising funds. The Trust
purchased this building on Locust Street in 1906, a four-story Greek Revival–style
brick townhouse with white marble trim. Renovations began to reconfigure the second floor into an auditorium with a stage for programs and classes. The Noon Rest
room and a kitchen were built, offering low-cost, nutritious meals to the members.
It also provided a place where women working in the city could find an affordable
and respectable place to have lunch. It created a lending library for members, and
temporary lodging on the third and fourth floors where members could stay over-
night for up to three nights a week for as little as 25 cents. The lodging offered a safe

place to spend the night and an opportunity for single working women to enjoy city life without the long commute home each night. They provided support for members, including emergency financial assistance, use of a hospital bed, and life insurance at a time when these opportunities were seldom available for working women. Membership also offered a network of like-minded women whose experiences in the workplace and interests in politics set them apart from their peers. Women often remained members throughout their working life and after retirement and the guild continued to offer a variety of activities for every interest. The building was designated a National Historic Landmark in 1993.

In 2018 the New Century Trust moved its headquarters into the Friends Center, part of the Race Street Meeting House (see related entry), and it continues to focus its work on improving the lives of women and girls. The trust uses its financial assets to support organizations working to remove barriers and create economic and political opportunities for women and girls in Philadelphia through grants and investments. The owner of this building on Locust Street is committed to preserving its history and its association with the New Century Guild. The west elevation of the building features a mural, "Women of Progress," that includes over 44 symbolic images representing diverse communities of women, the different roles they have played over time, and the complex obstacles they've overcome.

Pearl S. Buck House
520 Dublin Rd., Perkasie; (215) 249-0100; pearlsbuck.org; open year-round for guided tours; admission charged

A walk through the stone farmhouse at Green Hills Farm reveals a rich, almost intact collection of the life and work of author Pearl S. Buck. From the typewriter used to write *The Good Earth*, which sits on the desk in her office, to a closet full of board games ready for play, this home serves as a visual biography.

Pearl Comfort Sydenstricker was born in 1892, a child of Presbyterian missionaries in China. She grew up among the Chinese people, completely immersed in their culture. These experiences were the basis of her many novels that richly depicted Chinese village life.

In 1917 she married John Buck, an American agricultural missionary. The couple spent their first five years in a small town in China. In 1920 Pearl gave birth to her only biological child, Carol. With concern over the child's slow development, and very little support from her husband or doctors, she sought a place that could care for Carol, who was eventually diagnosed with a genetic disorder that resulted in progressive mental deterioration. Worried about paying for this care, she began writing in the hope that she could earn enough money to support Carol's institutional care.

After many rejections, her first book, *East Wind, West Wind*, was published in 1930 by Richard Walsh of the John Day Publishing Company. Her next book, *The Good Earth*, was a critical and financial success, earning her the Pulitzer Prize in 1932. A prolific writer, she penned 46 novels and over 1,000 other works.

In 1932 the Bucks returned to the United States. Pearl spent most of her time in New York City as a best-selling author and desired guest at parties, dinners, and lectures, but she craved a place in the country where she could write. She purchased Green Hills Farm, the first house she visited. She said the solid stone symbolized strength and durability. The original farmhouse was built in 1835. She made extensive alterations and additions to the house and remodeled the interior.

While the house was being renovated, Pearl and her publisher, Richard Walsh, developed a more personal relationship. Pearl divorced Buck and married Walsh in 1935. They raised a large international family including their seven adopted children and several foster children in this house.

Building on her literary themes and financial successes, Pearl turned her efforts to humanitarian causes. Her experiences in China led to her advocacy work in racial harmony as a means to achieving world peace. The Pearl S. Buck Foundation was formed in 1964 with a mission to provide aid to children throughout the world.

Pearl Buck maintained Green Hills Farm as her main residence from 1933 until her death in 1973. It was designated a National Historic Landmark in 1980. The

grounds of the estate contain her gravesite, greenhouse, and gardens, as well as the offices of Pearl S. Buck International, owners of the property.

Pennsylvania Academy of the Fine Arts
118-128 North Broad St., Philadelphia; (215) 972-2089; pafa.org; open Tues through Sun, year-round; admission charged

Founded in 1805 by painter Charles Willson Peale, sculptor William Rush, other artists, and business leaders, the Pennsylvania Academy of Fine Arts (PAFA) promoted the appreciation of the fine arts in the United States. It was the first art school in the United States with a list of graduates including distinguished painters and sculptors. Thomas Eakins, one of the most important artists in American art history, was a member of the faculty in the 1880s. The faculty continues to include some of the best artists of the time.

In 1845 a disastrous fire destroyed the east and north wings of the original PAFA building on Chestnut Street and resulted in the loss of a portion of their collection. Supporters rallied and raised the money for a new building that opened in 1847. When the leaders of PAFA were ready to build a larger home for their treasured collection, they directed architects Frank Furness and George Hewitt to design a building according to the specifications of "a two story, fireproof building with top-lighted galleries of varying sizes on the upper floor, all accessible from the main stair; and a lower floor containing library, lecture room, galleries for casts, and a painting room well lighted from a window close to the ceiling." The building on North Broad Street,

opened in 1876, was finished in time to be a highlight of the Philadelphia Centennial Exhibition, the first World's Fair in the United States. It is considered one of the best of Frank Furness's work and is the only well-preserved building of his that remains. The elaborate design includes a broad polychrome facade that is centered with an ornate, deeply recessed Gothic window above a double entrance. It is a chaotic mix of materials—brownstone, sandstone, polished granite, and red and black brick—that work together to convey the exuberance of the Victorian era.

PAFA has expanded to multiple buildings along Broad Street, and the 1876 building now houses the museum. Over the years this building has been altered and some of its opulence was toned down or covered. In the mid-1970s a restoration project rebuilt the entrance and vestibule, restored the interior wood, and repainted the elegant details, including gold rosettes and silver leaf stars. The interior color scheme was returned to its

Victorian palette. The drywall paneling that covered the iron and bronze columns in the rotunda was removed. The building was fully restored to its original grandeur. It was designated a National Historic Landmark in 1975.

The museum houses one of the best collections of American art in the United States. It explores the history of art in America from the 1760s to the present with a collection arranged in chronological and thematic formats. The Pennsylvania Academy of the Fine Arts is the oldest art school and art museum in the United States and continues to train future generations of artists and collect the works of contemporary artists.

Pennsylvania Hospital
800 Spruce St., Philadelphia; (215) 829-3370; pennmedicine.org/ for-patients-and-visitors/penn-medicine-locations/pennsylvania -hospital; guided tours available by appointment; no admission charged

The nation's oldest public hospital was conceived by Dr. Thomas Bond, a Philadelphia physician, who wanted to create a place to care for the sick, injured, and insane. He was unsuccessful in raising the needed funds, so he turned to Benjamin Franklin for assistance. The successful combined efforts of Bond and Franklin spurred some of the leading citizens of Philadelphia to file a petition with the Pennsylvania Colony's legislature in 1751 to request the funds to build the facility. Many legislators

opposed the plan as too expensive. When three physicians agreed to serve for three years without pay, the legislature approved the request and offered £2,000 ($3,600) if the petitioners could raise £2,000. They quickly raised £2,750 ($3,607) and reached out to Thomas and Richard Penn for a donation of a site to build the hospital.

The original building plan was designed in 1751 by Samuel Rhoads, a well-to-do builder. His plan called for a central building flanked by east and west wings. When the Penns would not agree to donate the site, a smaller lot was purchased in 1754. Because of the lack of funds and space, it was decided to construct only the east wing. The cornerstone was laid in 1755, and patients were first admitted in 1756. The wing is composed of a three-story square with a flat-roof and cupola, flanked on each side by two-and-one-half-story wings with hip roofs and dormers. Patients were segregated by floors with the "lunatic cells" in the basement, the men's ward on the first floor, the women's ward on the second floor, and the isolation cases in the attic.

Overcrowding was a serious problem, and the hospital planned its expansion using the adjacent ground that was donated to the hospital in 1767. The Commonwealth of Pennsylvania granted $26,000 to complete the original plan in 1794. The west wing, completed in 1796, duplicated the east wing. The central building, completed in 1802, is three and a half stories tall, with marble facing from the ground to the first story. Six pilasters reaching two full stories support a brick pediment with a fanlight. There is a hip roof with a central dome and skylight. Beneath the skylight is the first amphitheater in the United States, used to perform surgeries until 1868.

The hospital continued to grow, and many later buildings are part of the large hospital complex now. The historic portion of the hospital (now the Pine Building) survives remarkably unchanged and is open to the public. It contains the great court on the first floor, a second-floor historic library, and the original surgical amphitheater on the third floor. The building was designated a National Historic Landmark in 1965.

The Pennsylvania Hospital is owned and operated by Penn Medicine. They continue to preserve and showcase this historic building, offering guided tours of the facilities.

Pennsylvania State Capitol Complex
Commonwealth Ave., Harrisburg; (800) 868-7672; pacapitol.com; open year-round, guided tours daily; no admission charged

The Pennsylvania State Capitol is often referred to as a "Palace of Art," as it features paintings, stained glass, tiles, and furnishings of some of the best artisans at the time of its construction. After moving from Philadelphia to Lancaster, the seat of Pennsylvania government moved to Harrisburg. The present capitol is the third building on the current site. The Colonial or "Redbrick" Capitol, designed by Stephen Hills, was constructed between 1819 and 1822 at a cost of $135,000. In 1897 a fire broke out and within hours the dome had collapsed and the building was in ruins.

A new building, designed by architect Henry Ives Cobb, was quickly built in 1898 for $550,000. The structure was considered undignified and unattractive and was never completed. In 1901 a design competition awarded architect John Huston the commission for a third capitol that reused the outer walls of Cobb's design. The cornerstone was laid in 1904 and the building was dedicated in 1906. When President Theodore Roosevelt attended the dedication of the building, he said, "This is the handsomest building I ever saw."

The Pennsylvania State Capitol was designed in the Renaissance Revival style and was built and furnished for $13 million. The most striking feature is the 272-foot, 52-million-pound dome inspired by Michelangelo's design for St. Peter's Basilica in Rome. The dome is topped by a 14-foot-6-inch-high gilded statue of a female figure, *Commonwealth*. The five-story exterior is faced with Vermont granite, and the roof is covered in green-glazed terra-cotta tile. Each 17-foot door at the capitol's main entrance weighs a full ton but can easily swing open. The doors feature cast portrait heads of individuals responsible for the capitol's construction.

The interior rotunda contains a grand staircase and three-tiered gallery based on the Paris Opera House that is illuminated with 48 portholes in the dome and nearly 4,000 lights. The capitol contains 640 rooms. The art includes eight large murals by Philadelphia artist Edwin Austin Abbey in the rotunda in a tribute to Pennsylvania and its history. The 24 stained-glass windows in the Senate and House chambers were created by Philadelphia native William B. Van Ingen, a student of Louis C.

Tiffany and feature the themes of Architecture, Commerce, Education, History, Justice, Liberty, and Peace. Colorful Moravian tiles cover the first floor of the rotunda and its adjacent corridors and are one of the most impressive features of the capitol. Designed and manufactured by Henry Chapman Mercer of Doylestown, the floor is interspersed with close to 400 tile mosaics illustrating the state's history, animals, industries, occupations, and modes of transportation and is the largest single collection of Mercer tiles (see related entry).

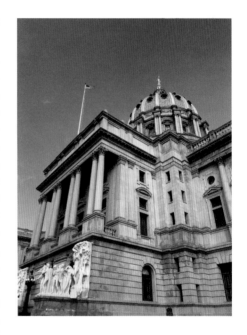

The capitol is owned by the Commonwealth of Pennsylvania. In 1982 the Pennsylvania Capitol Preservation Committee was formed to oversee the ongoing restoration and preservation of the art, architecture, and history of the complex. It was designated a National Historic Landmark in 2006, on the 100th anniversary of its dedication.

Philadelphia City Hall
1400 John F. Kennedy Blvd., Philadelphia; (215) 686-2840; phila .gov/virtualch; open weekdays year-round; free guided tours daily

Philadelphia City Hall is situated in the center of William Penn's original 1682 plans for the city, now known as Penn Square. The original seat of city government was a small two-story building, built in 1790, east of Independence Hall in Old City. When the City of Philadelphia doubled its population by consolidating with neighboring townships in 1854, a larger city hall was needed.

A design competition in 1869 awarded the prize to John McArthur Jr., a Philadelphia architect. Work began on the building in 1872 and was completed in 1901. McArthur designed a magnificent Second Empire–style building assisted by his design team of Philadelphia architect Thomas U. Walter—the designer of the dome on the US Capitol—and sculptor Alexander Milne Calder. With over 14 acres of floor space and almost 700 rooms, Philadelphia City Hall is the largest and most elaborate municipal building in the United States.

A square building encloses a central court that is linked to the streets by four monumental archways. The characteristic Second Empire features include the slate mansard roof with dormer windows, square-turreted courtyard stair towers, and paired columns that fool the eye into seeing the building as three stories instead of eight. The north facade is the ceremonial "front" of the building and the location of the 548-foot tower that terminates with a 37-foot-tall statue of William Penn. The visitor observation deck, right below the statue, is 40 stories above the ground. There are four 26-foot-diameter clocks on each side of the tower. In order to support the tower, the walls are 22 feet thick at the base. Built without a steel or iron frame, City Hall is one of the tallest all-masonry, load-bearing buildings in the world.

The interior and exterior of the building feature 250 sculptures, all created by Calder, depicting animals, continents, seasons, arts and sciences, heads, and masks. Four colossal bronze statues, each 24 feet tall weighing between 8 and 11 tons sit at the corners of the tower below the Penn statue. On each of the four faces of the tower, between the statues, is a bronze eagle with a wing spread of 12 feet. Throughout the building are hundreds more sculptures, reliefs, keystones, spandrels, panels, capitals, and medallions, in marble and bronze.

A wide corridor runs around each of the floors; every office has outside windows and opens on the corridor. There are staircases at every corner and four banks of elevators included in the original design. The interior's lavish materials and superior craftsmanship include polished marble, hand-carved woodwork, wrought-iron grilles, ornamental ceilings, and mosaic floors. The public rooms are the most lavish in the city.

A complete exterior restoration of City Hall began in 1992 and was completed by 2007. Four new ornamental courtyard gates were installed in 2015, based on original architectural sketches. The building was designated a National Historic Landmark in 1976 and a National Civil Engineering Landmark in 2006.

The Philadelphia Contributionship
210 S. Fourth St., Philadelphia; (215) 627-1752; 1752.com; museum open by appointment; no admission charged

In 1752 Benjamin Franklin founded and organized the Philadelphia Contributionship for the Insurance of Houses from Loss by Fire. It was the first fire insurance company in the United States and originated the practice of setting rates according to the determined risk. A mutual insurance company operates with policyholders sharing the risks of all, based on the Amicable Contributionship of London. Surveyors inspected each building prior to accepting it for coverage and the directors of the company would set rates based on risk. The contributionship became a pioneer in the development of the insurance industry across the nation and is the longest-operating insurance company in the country.

During its early years, the Philadelphia Contributionship had no permanent headquarters. The directors conducted the firm's general business during periodic meetings in various public buildings or taverns. Policyholders met annually in the Philadelphia Courthouse, and the company clerk carried out routine day-to-day business from his home or office.

In 1835 the directors wanted a permanent headquarters that would both house the treasurer and his family and serve as the business office. They commissioned Philadelphia architect Thomas U. Walter, known for his work in the Greek Revival style, to design a three-story brick building with a marble portico and a Corinthian entablature supported by four fluted Corinthian columns. In 1866 the portico was replaced, and a marble cornice and fourth story topped by a mansard roof was added. When the last treasurer's family moved out in 1898, the building was converted to full office use.

The building has served as the company's headquarters since its completion in 1836. A small museum area on the first floor showcases the company's key founding documents, a counting house desk, and an exhibit of fire marks and artifacts from Philadelphia's volunteer fire companies. The building was designated a National Historic Landmark in 1977.

Philadelphia Savings Fund Society Building
1200 W. Market St., Philadelphia; (215) 627-1200; loewshotels .com/philadelphia-hotel; open year-round; no admission charged

The Philadelphia Savings Fund Society (PSFS), headquartered in Philadelphia, was founded in December 1816, the first savings bank to organize and do business in the United States. Based on the popular savings banks in Great Britain, the bank organized with a goal to encourage everyone, including children, to open savings accounts. By 1910 it had the most depositors of any savings bank in the United States.

In the midst of the Great Depression, PSFS built a skyscraper of modern design for their corporate headquarters in center city Philadelphia. Determined to build a structure that would represent its past greatness and future leadership, the building committee, led by PSFS President James M. Willcox selected a bold, modern design submitted by George Howe and William Lescaze. Designed in the International Style, the sleek and streamlined 36-story building, with identical glass-walled

floors of office space, would wrap around a steel skeleton with a service tower rising the height of the building that formed a T-shaped spine. It was also the first building of its size to be fully air-conditioned year-round. The first level included shops, then three floors of banking offices with a luxurious executive suite on the top. Twenty-seven floors of leasable office space filled the remainder of the building. The architects also designed all the furniture, hardware, and fixtures to keep the sleek, ornament-free concept. The PSFS sign on top of the building, with red neon letters 27 feet high, can be seen for more than 20 miles on a clear night. It is one of Philadelphia's best-known beacons. The building was completed in 1932 at a total cost of $7.4 million.

The modern design was both loved and hated, some calling it hideous and repellent. In 1932 the Museum of Modern Art featured it in an exhibition of modern architecture, while Frank Lloyd Wright called it "neither international nor a style." Interestingly, Wright's Fallingwater (see related entry) was designed in the International Style only a few years later. PSFS architect William Howe formed a partnership with Louis Kahn, another Modernist architect. Together they collaborated on some of the most architecturally acclaimed Modernist buildings, including the Richards Medical Research Building (see related entry) at the University of Pennsylvania

In 1946 PSFS allowed a television station to construct a 256-foot transmission tower atop the building. This decision broke a long-standing gentlemen's agreement that no building or structure would rise higher than the statue of William Penn on City Hall. The addition of this tower increased the height of the building to 737 feet. The Philadelphia Savings Fund Society filed for bankruptcy in 1992 and became part of the Mellon Bank Company. The Loews Corporation bought the PSFS Building in 1997. It was remodeled into the Loews Philadelphia Hotel and reopened in April 2000. The PSFS sign is still in place and lights the night sky. The building was designated a National Historic Landmark in 1976.

Race Street Meetinghouse
**1515 Cherry St., Philadelphia; (215) 241-7100; friendscentercorp
.org; open year-round; no admission charged**

Among the major religious denominations in the 19th century, the Religious Society of Friends (Quakers) permitted the greatest role for women. They could contribute during meetings and worship services and were active in church government. Long before other denominations ordained women, the Quakers had women ministers. The Quakers' progressive attitude toward slavery encouraged Quaker women to take leadership roles in abolitionist, women's rights, and peace movements. Many leaders in the women's movement were associated with the Race Street Meetinghouse,

including abolitionist and women's activist Lucretia Mott, peace activist Hannah Clothier Hull, and suffrage leader Alice Paul.

The Race Street Meetinghouse, built in 1856, is a two-story brick building with a front-facing gabled roof containing an arched window. The seven-bay-wide facade has three doors separated by four 12-over-12 sash windows with paneled shutters on the first floor and seven 12-over-12 sash windows with louvered shutters on the second floor. The doorways are reached by four stone steps onto a porch with a simple cantilevered entablature. Originally the Race Street facade was the formal entrance to the building and was set back from the street to create a courtyard. The interior of the building contained two meeting rooms separated by a wide hallway with a central staircase. The northern meeting room was designed to house the Monthly Meeting and the Women's Yearly Meeting and the southern meeting room housed the Men's Yearly Meeting. By 1926 men and women were no longer meeting separately, so the room was converted to a social hall. The meetinghouse is still in active use.

The Race Street Meetinghouse served as the site of the Hicksite Yearly Meeting from 1857 to 1955. In 1827, due to an ideological controversy, Quakers split into two factions, Orthodox and Hicksite. Prior to the split, all Quakers in the greater Philadelphia area met annually for the Yearly Meeting at Arch Street Meetinghouse. When the Hicksites broke away from Orthodox Quakerism, they held their annual meetings at the Cherry Street Meetinghouse and eventually the Race Street Meetinghouse. In 1955 the Hicksite and Orthodox factions reconciled, and from that point on the Yearly Meeting was once again held in the Arch Street Meetinghouse.

In the early 1960s a group of Friends envisioned a place where Quakers could gather for thought and action. They created the Friends Center, where service organizations could be housed together. The site they chose incorporates the Race Street Meetinghouse and its tree-filled courtyard. On the east side of the meetinghouse, between the two meeting rooms, is a narrow connection to the modern Friends Center building, constructed in 1975. The complex is managed by the Friends Center Corporation. The Race Street Meetinghouse was designated a National Historic Landmark in 1993.

Reading Terminal Market and Train Shed
12th & Arch Sts., Philadelphia; (215) 922-2317; readingterminal market.org; open year-round; no admission charged

Completed in 1893, this structure is the largest single-span, arched-roof train shed in the world. A monument in engineering history, it once covered 13 tracks and 8 platforms. Its structure is a series of wrought-iron three-hinged arches that span a width of 259 feet and reach a height of 88 feet. The shed is 559 feet long. Utilitarian in style, it is attached to the rear of the more elaborate eight-story head house terminal that contained the waiting room and offices. Joseph M. Wilson designed the shed for the Philadelphia and Reading Railroad, and because viaducts brought trains into the station's second-floor level, he was able to incorporate a large market at street level.

The Reading Terminal Market opened for business in 1893 with the sounds of trains rumbling overhead. Stalls were laid out in a grid pattern, with 12 east–west aisles and 4 wider north–south aisles. The large cold-storage area in the basement required sawdust to be spread on the floors to help absorb the rising damp. By 1913, 250 food vendors and 100 farmers were doing business in the market. The Reading Terminal Market offered a state-of-the-art refrigeration system with 52 separate rooms occupying 500,000 cubic feet. Each room could be regulated to a specific temperature. The market offered free delivery service using boys called "market brats" who carried small orders to nearby customers. People living near train stations served by the Reading or Pennsylvania Railroads called in orders and had their goods dropped at stations near their homes.

During the Great Depression of the 1930s, Reading Terminal Market served an important role. Compared to other businesses, the market prospered because local farmers could bring their merchandise to a city where supply was scarce and prices were good. During World War II, small local farmers sold their goods to customers at the market who waited in long lines with their ration books. Ninety-seven percent of the stalls were occupied, even in 1944. In the 1960s the railroad business was suffering an economic downturn. The market was forced to close its refrigeration system, and stand holders had to purchase their own walk-in refrigeration units. In 1971 a severe cash shortage and declining freight and passenger traffic finally forced the railroad company into bankruptcy.

In 1990 the Pennsylvania Convention Center Authority purchased the market and train shed from the Reading Railroad Company. The Authority and the merchants negotiated preservation agreements and secured $30 million for market infrastructure. In 1995 the Authority created a nonprofit corporation to manage the market.

The Reading Terminal Market is home to more than 80 merchants, 2 of whom are descendants of the original stand holders. Reading Terminal Market is open every day and serves 100,000 customers each week. The train shed has been incorporated into the Philadelphia Convention Center. The Reading Terminal building was designated a National Historic Landmark in 1976.

Schaeffer House
213 S. Carpenter St., Schaefferstown; (717) 949-2244; hsimuseum .org/museums; open by appointment; admission charged

The Alexander Schaeffer House is an important example of an 18th-century Colonial German–style house built prior to 1737. Constructed of coursed rubble limestone, the original house had two rooms on the first floor, a kitchen, and a parlor. Shortly after its construction, a bed chamber was added, giving it the more

traditional three-room German configuration. Alexander Schaeffer purchased the house in 1758 and enlarged it in 1771 with a two-story addition, transforming it into a Weinbauernhaus, a European traditional style structure that combines living quarters and the production of alcoholic beverages in a single building. This house is banked, allowing access to the house on both the ground floor where a vaulted area was used to store alcohol and access to the living and distilling space above from the top of the banked hill. A large kitchen on the upper level housed the still, and the fireplace was adapted for use in the distilling process. Schaeffer probably acquired this property in order to provide spirits for a tavern he operated on the main road in town.

In 1758, Schaeffer laid out the town of Heidelberg, named after a town in his native Germany. He used his knowledge of German towns to plan Heidelberg situated around a central square and began selling lots. He kept the best lot for himself near the center of town where he built and operated a general store and tavern, named the King George Hotel (renamed the Franklin House after the American Revolution and still operating). The locals began calling the town Schaeffer's Town and eventually the name Schaefferstown was formally adopted.

Two main roads lined with homes and business intersect at the center square. Schaefferstown became an important crossroads community with the east-west road running between Ephrata and the Cornwall Iron Furnace in the east and Harris's Ferry (Harrisburg) to the west. The north-south road connected the settlement laid out by Conrad Weiser (Tulpehocken) to the north and Lancaster to the south. The settlement was an excellent location to provide goods and services to the many travelers who passed through and the town grew into a busy center of commerce.

Schaeffer devised a system of underground wooden pipes to provide water to the town. Connected to a strong spring at the south of end of Market Street, water flowed uphill toward center square where it filled two troughs on the town square. Schaeffer deeded the reservoir property (now known as Fountain Park) and the water system to the residents of Market Street. Homeowners on that street are automatically members of the Schaefferstown Water Company, whose responsibility it is to maintain the park and the two "fountains." One trough on the square was replaced in 1910 with a granite fountain, donated by the great-granddaughter of Alexander Schaeffer.

Schaeffer married Anna Engel in 1738 and together they had seven children. He died in 1786 at the age of 74. The Alexander Schaeffer House is located on an 85-acre farm southwest of Schaefferstown. It is owned by Historic Schaefferstown, Inc., a nonprofit dedicated to the culture and history of the area. The house is operated as a historic site and is a rare surviving example of the European tradition of combining both residential and manufacturing activities under one roof. The house was designated a National Historic Landmark in 2011.

Second Bank of the United States
420 Chestnut St., Philadelphia; (215) 965-2305; nps.gov/inde/ learn/historyculture/places-secondbank.htm; open year-round; hours vary with season; no admission charged

The Second Bank of the United States was first established in Carpenters' Hall in 1817 (see related entry). In the hope of avoiding another financial crisis like the one that occurred during the War of 1812, Congress established the first federal bank. The large war debt demanded that something be done to restore order to the chaotic state of American finance. Without a central financial institution, it was difficult for the government to repay loans. Foreign credit was in poor standing, there was no uniform national currency, and bank notes could not be exchanged for gold. The First Bank of the United States (see related entry) operated between 1791 and 1811 as the first national bank. Not without controversy, Congress did not renew the charter in 1811. This forced the government to finance the war effort through a private bank, and when the war ended, there was no way to pay back the loan.

As a result, many Americans who opposed the First Bank changed their minds and supported the establishment of the Second Bank of the United States. After a shaky start, the Second Bank settled down to become a conservative, prosperous,

and reasonably responsible business enterprise. Under the leadership of Nicholas Biddle, the institution soon became an effective regulator of the national economy.

Although the constitutionality of a national bank seemed to have been settled during the establishment of the First Bank, President Andrew Jackson criticized it repeatedly during his first term in office, saying that the Second Bank was unconstitutional and dangerous to republican ideals. In 1832 Jackson's political opponents made it an election issue by forcing an early renewal of the bank's 20-year charter. The plan backfired when Jackson vetoed the bill. The Second Bank's funds were transferred to state banks by 1836.

Jackson's veto made it clear that the Supreme Court was not the final arbiter of constitutional matters and that the president could exercise a judgment, independent of Congress. This led to the growth of the system of checks and balances in the relationship between the executive, legislative, and judicial branches of government.

The building was designed by architect William Strickland and built between 1819 and 1824 at a cost of nearly $500,000. Modeled after the Parthenon in Athens, it is an excellent example of Greek Revival architecture. A marble set of stairs lead to a portico with fluted Doric columns and entablature. After the bank closed in 1836, the building became the Custom House that resulted in many interior changes. However, the banking room, the heart of the building, retains its two rows of Ionic columns and its barrel-vaulted ceiling. This room now houses a gallery featuring over 150 portraits of 18th- and 19th-century political leaders, including over 100 portraits by Charles Willson Peale.

In 1948 Congress added the building to Independence National Historical Park. Owned and operated by the National Park Service, it was designated a National Historic Landmark in 1987.

Simon Cameron House
219 S. Front St., Harrisburg; (717) 233-3462; dauphincountyhistory .org/museum; open year-round; admission charged

The Simon Cameron House was designated a National Historic Landmark in 1975 but its history began long before Cameron was associated with it. In the early 1700s, John Harris Sr., received a large land grant from the Penn family, establishing a trading post and a ferry service on the banks of the Susquehanna River, leading to the settlement of Harrisburg.

After his father's death, in order to avoid the constant flooding problem near the river, John Jr., selected higher ground, farther away from the river, to build a more substantial house. In 1766 he built the front section of the current limestone house. It remained in the family until 1835. Sometime during this period the rear wing was added. In 1853 the house was sold to the Reverend Beverly Waugh and his wife, who converted it into the Pennsylvania Female College. The turmoil of the Civil War forced the school into bankruptcy only a few years later.

Simon Cameron, a member of the college's board of directors, was a self-made man who had accumulated a large fortune through a combination of hard work, investments, and, some said, unethical business practices. He offered $8,000 for the house.

Cameron had a long and storied political career, serving a total of 20 years in the US Senate in nonconsecutive terms starting in 1845. When he failed to secure a nomination for a second term from the Know-Nothing Party (American Party), he joined the People's Party (later the Republican Party). He won the Senate seat in 1857. When he did not receive the Republican nomination for the 1860 presidential election, Cameron gave his support to Abraham Lincoln and served under Lincoln as his secretary of war, resigning after one year amid allegations of corruption.

In 1862 Cameron became the minister to Russia. Having made the offer on the house prior to his departure, he traveled throughout Europe shopping for furnishings. In the parlor are two 14-foot-tall pier mirrors from France and twin hand-carved Italian marble fireplace mantles. Colored-glass in the windows was imported from Bavaria.

Cameron resigned his post in Russia in 1863. He returned to the United States and transformed the house into the popular Victorian-era Italianate style. He added a solarium, walkway, butler's pantry, and grand staircase. He also lowered the floor 3 feet into the basement in the front section of the house to accommodate his new 14-foot mirrors.

In 1867 Cameron was again elected to the Senate, serving 10 more years and securing the seat for his son to succeed him in 1877. Throughout his career he used his power to his advantage and built a powerful Republican Party that

continued to dominate politics after his death. In 1889 the house passed to his daughter and eventually was donated by the family to the Historical Society in 1941. The John Harris-Simon Cameron Mansion is owned and operated by the Historical Society of Dauphin County.

USS *Olympia*
211 S. Columbus Blvd., Philadelphia; (215) 729-5281; phillyseaport .org/olympia; open year-round; admission charged

In 1898 Commodore George Dewey, aboard the Flagship *Olympia*, led a squadron of state-of-the-art steel warships into Manila Bay in the Philippines. In the early morning of May 1, Dewey ordered Captain Charles Gridley to open fire using the famous line, "You may fire when ready Gridley." Within two and a half hours, the Spanish force was destroyed.

The *Olympia* and Commodore Dewey achieved great notoriety after the victory at Manila Bay. At the end of the Spanish-American War, *Olympia* led a parade in New York Harbor, firing salutes from all her guns. Newspapers across the country printed images of the *Olympia* with detailed descriptions of the battle. Popular magazines rans photos and illustrations of the now-famous ship. Souvenirs, including clocks, mirrors, lamps, and lithographs, were produced and sold across the country with images of the *Olympia* in full color.

The USS *Olympia*, built by the Union Iron Works of San Francisco from 1890 to 1893, was the largest of four new protected cruisers. The protected cruiser was a new type of navy vessel that included an armored deck that protected its machinery from exploding shells. With twin triple-expansion engines, she was faster than any previous US cruiser. Her cruising range was 6,000 miles. The hull of the ship was white with a red stripe at its waterline and a buff topside. The bow of the ship was very pointed, like a knife, to allow for ramming enemy ships and other water vessels. It was 344 feet in length and weighed 5,500 tons. The interior was elegant. The ship's wooden main deck was painted a glossy magenta and included well-maintained compartments for enlisted men, with worn mess tables and hammocks. The Victorian appointments in the admiral's and captain's staterooms and quarters made them seem more like an English manor house with a piano, porcelain bathtubs, fine china cabinets, and oak paneling.

For the rest of her commissioned life, *Olympia* would be a symbol of America's emerging power even after being surpassed in speed, protection, and weaponry. During World War I, the *Olympia* was painted gray, and the decorations were removed to become part of a display in Annapolis. But she continued to complete missions, still a strong symbol of the power of the Navy. Her last mission was the transport of the Unknown Soldier from France back home to America.

Olympia is the last ship remaining of the "Great White Fleet" and is also the sole surviving combatant of the Spanish-American War. Now retired and restored to its 1898 appearance, the *Olympia* is moored at Penn's Landing and is owned by the Independence Seaport Museum. She was designated a National Historic Landmark in 1964. In 2016, in cooperation with the museum, the Flagship *Olympia* Foundation formed to raise funds for the restoration and preservation of the *Olympia*.

Valley Forge National Historical Park and Washington's Headquarters
1400 N. Outer Line Dr., King of Prussia; (610) 783-1000; nps.gov/ vafo; open year-round; no admission charged

In November 1777 General William Howe and the British forces were securely settled in Philadelphia for the winter, leaving George Washington and the Continental Army camped north of Philadelphia in tents. The capture of Philadelphia removed the Continental Army's source of supplies and their planned winter quarters. Washington was faced with the decision to recapture Philadelphia or seek winter camp elsewhere. The Continental Congress threated to withdraw men, supplies, and financial aid if the army did not remain close to Philadelphia. Washington chose Valley Forge, a small community west of Philadelphia. The march to Valley Forge

was rigorous, and they were delayed by several skirmishes. It took eight days for 11,000 men to complete the 15-mile journey, many of them shoeless, shirtless, and sick.

Using the natural defense of the Schuylkill River to the north, an inner and outer line of defense was constructed. The inner line was a series of earthworks forming a semicircle from the northwest to the southwest along a ridgeline. The earthworks were supported by the Star Redoubt (fort), Fort Huntington, and Fort Washington. Just forward of the inner line, a fortification of sharply pointed rails, timbers, and saplings was erected. To the east of the inner line stretched the outer line of defense, which ran roughly east to west with parallel lines of earthworks and trenches and two redoubts at its eastern terminus. The area bounded by the lines of defense contained the bulk of the encampment. The 900 soldiers' and officers' huts were located directly behind the trenches. The grand parade ground was located on a flat plane just south of the Star Redoubt.

By Christmas Eve most of the huts had been completed, and Washington moved from his tent into a small stone house on the bank of Valley Creek. This stone farmhouse served as Washington's headquarters from Christmas Eve 1777 to June 1778. From February through June, Martha Washington left the comforts of Mount Vernon to join her husband here. The house features an elaborate Georgian interior. His general officers took up residence with many of the local families in the surrounding countryside. The conditions were significantly better than tents in open fields, but it was a rough winter with a lack of clothing and food that contributed to illness and death for 2,500 men.

The highpoint of the occupation was the arrival of Baron von Steuben, former professional soldier who joined the American cause. He drilled the troops and began to develop Washington's men into trained soldiers who would eventually defeat the British. By spring the Continental Army was strong, and in June 1778 they reoccupied Philadelphia.

Valley Forge is now a National Historical Park operated by the National Park Service. It contains many original buildings, including Washington's headquarters and replicas of the soldiers' huts. A variety of tours are offered throughout the 3,500-acre park. Valley Forge was declared a National Historic Landmark in 1961, and Washington's Headquarters was designated in 1972.

Wagner Free Institute of Science

1700 W. Montgomery Ave., Philadelphia; (215) 763-6529; wagnerfreeinstitute.org; open year-round Tues through Fri; admission charged

Founded in 1855, the Wagner Free Institute of Science is a rare surviving example of a Victorian-era scientific society. Philadelphia merchant, philanthropist, and amateur scientist William Wagner opened this private museum, research center, library, and educational facility to exhibit his personal collection of natural history

specimens gathered on his travels. His personal mineral collection, one of the oldest in the country, and his extensive fossil collection have been on display since the museum opened in 1865. The regional entomology collection still includes the handwritten curator's labels.

The most striking feature of the museum is an open three-story exhibit hall containing a collection of mounted birds and mammals, shells, and dinosaur bones. In 1886 a museum-sponsored trip to Florida included the discovery of the first saber-toothed tiger in America, which is now included in the display. Artifacts are displayed in cherry-wood and glass cabinets and maintain their original layout providing a rare view of a Victorian-era science museum. The exhibits represent one of the largest systematically arranged collections on display in the country. The collections are still in active use as a key educational tool of the institute's free science programs and a resource for scholarly research.

The Wagner Free Institute's commitment to preservation extended to its historic heating system in 2011. The early-20th-century steam-vapor heating system was state-of-the-art in its day. Patented in 1906, the Broomell Vapor Heating System became one of the most extensively used heating systems for residential, commercial, and institutional buildings. The institute was outfitted with a Broomell heating plant in 1907, and it may be one of the earliest surviving buildings with this technology still operational. When faced with boiler replacement, a plan was designed to restore the existing system, removing modifications that were not compatible and introducing high-performance, high-efficiency boilers and controls. The project reflects the

institute's long-standing commitment to maintaining the historic integrity of its site. It demonstrates that green design and sustainable practices can be incorporated into a historic building without compromising preservation standards.

Remarkably the institute is nearly unchanged from the 19th century. It remains the oldest program devoted to free adult education in the US. With its commitment to preserving the historic integrity of the building and its collections, it is recognized as a "museum of a museum." The Wagner Free Institute of Science provides free public education in science through a wide array of programs for adults and children, including evening science courses, public lectures by leading scientists and scholars, and field trips for school groups. It was designated a National Historic Landmark in 1990.

Washington's Crossing
1112 River Rd., Washington Crossing; (215) 493-4076; washingtoncrossingpark.org; open year-round; fee for guided tours

By December 1776, the War for Independence was not going well for the Continental Army. General George Washington's campaign in New York was a failure, and he was forced to retreat through New Jersey into Pennsylvania in early December. With hunger and lack of supplies taking their toll on his diminishing numbers of soldiers, Washington needed a victory. He planned a risky nighttime crossing of the Delaware River and a march to Trenton to attack Hessian outposts. Washington's troops gathered boats that could be used to make the dangerous crossing, specifically large, heavy Durham boats used to carry pig iron down the Delaware.

Washington assembled his troops near McConkey's Ferry and by 6:00 p.m., on December 25, 1776, 2,400 troops began crossing the river. The river was full of ice, and travel was brutal. They fought their way through sleet and a blinding snowstorm. Washington expected two supporting divisions to join him on the opposite shore, but both abandoned their crossings because of the conditions. On the morning of December 26, Washington and his troops marched to Trenton and won victory over the Hessians. This spurred new support for the cause of freedom.

The first commemoration of the crossing occurred in 1854 when the railroad stop on the New Jersey side was named Washington Crossing. State parks were established on both banks of the river, in New Jersey in 1912 and in Pennsylvania in 1917. The village near the site in Pennsylvania was given the name Washington

Crossing in 1919. Washington Crossing Historic Park contains 500 acres and is owned by the Commonwealth of Pennsylvania and managed by the Department of Conservation and Natural Resources. The Friends of Washington Crossing Park operate the site and offer a variety of activities throughout the year. Most popular is the December reenactment of Washington's Christmas crossing. Washington Crossing was designated a National Historic Landmark in 1972.

Wharton Esherick House and Studio
1520 Horseshoe Trl., Malvern; (610) 644-5822; whartonesherickmuseum.org; open year-round for guided tours, reservations required; admission charged

Recognized as a leader in nontraditional design, Wharton Esherick's work exemplifies his motto, "If it isn't fun, it isn't worth doing." A Philadelphia native, Esherick began his training at the Pennsylvania Museum School of Industrial Arts, where he studied drawing and printmaking. In 1913, after studying painting at the Pennsylvania Academy of Fine Arts (see related entry), he moved to the country and began his painting career. His interest in wood began in 1920 with the carving of simple designs on frames for his paintings. This led to carving woodcuts—some 350 blocks and 9 illustrated books—and carving on furniture. In the 1920s Esherick became fascinated with the nature of wood. He began sculpting and fully explored the many qualities of wood and used it in ways that had never been done. By 1926 his sculpture was exhibited at the Whitney Museum of American Art in New York City. Continuing to seek new ways to work with this material, he turned to interiors, designing the interior of a home for Curtis Bok, a Pennsylvania Supreme Court judge. When the house was demolished, the fireplace, adjacent music room doors, and foyer stairs were salvaged and installed in the Philadelphia Museum of Art.

His studio, built between 1926 and 1966, is his largest piece of art. It showcases the evolution of his work from the Arts and Crafts period through the Modernist period. Every feature of the building, from the door handles and light pulls to the carved staircase that is considered a functional sculpture, were designed and built by Esherick. The red-oak staircase, completed in 1930, spirals from his workshop to his bedroom loft, twisting as it rises with a section that looks like the piston in a

rotary engine. The treads are carved with broad, quick strokes that give them faced edges, showing off the grain of the wood. Each tread has a tenon that fits into mortises on the stair shaft and is locked in place by a furniture bolt. The staircase can be dismantled and has been taken out of the house twice. In 1940 the staircase, along with some of his furniture, was used to create an exhibit at the New York World's Fair.

Close to the studio is an unusual collaboration between Esherick, known for his smooth sculptural lines, and Louis Kahn, known for his angles and geometric shapes, known as the 1956 Workshop. Both men had strong personalities, finally compromising on a plan that was essentially three joined hexagons and three diamond-shaped roof planes with sloping eaves, an interesting marriage of their two design styles. The date of construction and their initials are carved by the front door.

Esherick continued to work on the studio until his death in 1970. In 1972 it was converted into the Wharton Esherick Museum. A 1928 German Expressionist log garage, also designed by Esherick, now serves as a visitor center. The collection of buildings, including the studio, workshop, and garage, was declared a National Historic Landmark in 1993. The property is owned and operated by the Wharton Esherick Museum, a private nonprofit organization.

The Woodlands

4000 Woodland Ave., Philadelphia; (215) 386-2181; woodlandsphila.org; grounds open year-round, no admission charged; mansion tours available on Thurs (Apr through Oct), admission charged

William Hamilton (1745–1813) was born in Philadelphia to a wealthy family of lawyers and politicians. At age 21, he inherited over 300 acres of land on the west side of the Schuylkill River. He built a Georgian house (c. 1770) with a two-story columned portico overlooking the water. After the American Revolution, Hamilton traveled to England and visited grand country estates. Between 1786 and 1789 he expanded his house in the Adams (Federal) style, popular in England at the time. The completed building is symmetrically balanced with a Doric-columned portico on the south and a formal terrace on the north. The reworked first floor contains three rooms of different shapes accessed off the domed vestibule. The house is two stories in height with a finished attic and basement. To keep the activities of servants out of the view of his guests, he built the kitchen and service facilities in the basement with passages that radiate out from a servant's vestibule in the center. Access to the basement is through a cryptoporticus (a covered passageway) located under the terrace on the north side.

Hamilton was an eminent botanist and plant collector, and the Woodlands gardens were based on the gardens of the English countryside. His plant collection included 10,000 species, and he boasted that "there was not a plant in Europe, Asia, Africa, from China and the islands in the South Sea . . . which he had not procured." He used his connections to obtain rare plants from his neighbors John Penn Jr. and John Bartram (see related entry), and he successfully lobbied to receive seeds sent by Lewis and Clark from their trip to the Pacific in 1804 to 1806.

The establishment of the Woodlands Cemetery Company on the site in 1840 began the slow transformation of Hamilton's garden into a rural cemetery. William Hamilton's home remained the centerpiece, serving both ceremonial and functional purposes. The house and its original English gardens provided the inspiration for the development of the cemetery and still defines it as a rather unique cultural landscape.

An interesting feature of the cemetery are the many cradle graves, popular in the Victorian era. A cradle grave provides a place for planting flowers and consists of a headstone, footstone, and two low walls connecting them. In the middle there is a place where family members can plant and maintain small flower gardens. When the cemetery was established, it was common for people to maintain these gardens and spend time there on the weekends enjoying peaceful green space outside of the city. The Woodlands Grave Gardeners is a volunteer gardening program that is reintroducing this practice by pairing volunteer gardeners with flowerless graves.

The Woodlands is a nonprofit organization with a mission to preserve and interpret the 54-acre site that includes the mansion, the landscape, and the cemetery. The Woodland Cemetery Company was established in 1840 and is still an active burial ground. The site was designated a National Historic Landmark in 1967.

Woodmont
1622 Spring Mill Rd., Gladwyne; (610) 525-5598; peacemission .info/father-divine; open Sun (Apr through Oct); weekday tours by appointment; modest dress required; no admission charged

Architect William Lightfoot Price designed Woodmont, and it was built in the 1890s for industrialist Alan Wood Jr., one of the founders of the Alan Wood Iron and Steel Company. Price had impressed Wood with his personal knowledge of the building that was to be Woodmont's model, Biltmore, the George W. Vanderbilt house in Asheville, North Carolina. Under construction since 1889, Biltmore had already attracted considerable attention as America's most expensive private house. Price was in Ashville building the Kenilworth Inn, a project financed by Strawbridge & Clothier of Philadelphia and Vanderbilt.

Price designed Woodmont to resemble a French chateau with turrets, towers, oriel windows, and gargoyles. It is oriented east and west and set parallel to the ridge above the Schuylkill River. Approached from the south, the house is an assembly of steep gabled and hipped roofs and a boldly projecting porte cochere, all of which are dominated by the high pyramidal roof of the Great Hall at the center of the

building. A polygonal porch with a conical roof, now enclosed as a room, terminates the west end of the facade. Construction is entirely of local schist, lightly rusticated and relieved with extensive trim and architectural sculpture in Indiana limestone, including the moldings, belt courses, and finials. The roof is variegated red tiles with copper coverings for dormer roofs and turret caps. Ornamental copper cresting framed by needle-thin spires accentuate the height of the roof peaks.

Alan Wood Jr., occupied the estate for less than a decade. A year before his death in 1902, he sold it to his nephew, Richard G. Wood, who lived there for 28 years. In 1929 Richard subdivided the land, selling 200 acres to the Philadelphia Country Club. In 1952 the Reverend M. J. Divine, better known as Father Divine, made Woodmont his home and the headquarters of the Peace Mission Movement of Father and Mother Divine. An African-American charismatic preacher, Father Divine became widely known in the 1930s as the leader of a progressive religious and social movement that embraced integration long before the national Civil Rights Movement. Father Divine is buried on the property, which is open to the public.

The property is owned by Palace Mission Church, Inc. It was designated a National Historic Landmark in 1998.

Wyck House
6026 Germantown Ave., Philadelphia; (215) 848-1690; wyck.org; open Fri through Sun (Apr through mid-Nov); admission charged

Hans Millan, a German immigrant to Germantown, built a small house in 1690. Wyck was subsequently enlarged, rebuilt, and lived in by nine generations of his family. The stone house, furnishings, and a rare collection of family papers survive to provide a portrait of an American family's way of life through two centuries.

Dirk Jansen (c. 1680–1760), married to Millan's daughter, likely built the two-and-one-half-story house that now forms the western end of Wyck. The stone building had a three-room plan dominated by a central chimney. Jansen also built a smaller house 18 feet closer to Germantown Avenue, the south wall of which aligned perfectly with the south wall of the large house. The floor plan consisted of a single room with a small chimney on the north wall and the entrance on the south wall.

In 1771 Reuben Haines I (1727–1793) connected the two houses with a two-and-a-half-story addition. The original floor plans of both houses were retained, permitting their use as separate dwellings for the next 50 years. The first floor of the connecting section was left open, as a breezeway and the second floor had a single bedroom. During the Battle of Germantown in 1777, the building was used as a hospital for the British army. By the 1790s the breezeway between the houses was enclosed to form the hall, with large paneled doors that could be opened for cross-ventilation.

Yellow fever epidemics devastated Philadelphia in the 1790s, killing about one-seventh of the population. Philadelphians escaped into Germantown to benefit from the higher elevation and fresh air. The Wyck property was inherited by Reuben Haines's son Caspar (1762–1801), after his parents died nursing yellow fever victims in 1793. Caspar Haines, a wealthy brewer from Philadelphia, built the Germantown Brewery 100 feet north of his house in 1794.

In 1820 Reuben Haines III, son of Caspar, moved to Germantown with his wife Jane. Rueben updated the house with the help of William Strickland, architect of the Second Bank of the United States (see related entry). Few changes were made to the exterior, but he blended the interiors of the two houses into a single mansion that made good use of space and light. He created larger rooms and converted the hall into a room that was sunny year-round by installing sliding doors with glass panes. The house transformed into an elegant country house, and three generations of their descendants devoted much of their lives to its preservation. The house was designated a National Historic Landmark in 1990.

In 1973 the Haines family, realizing the value of Wyck, gave the property to the Wyck Charitable Trust. The Wyck Association manages the preservation and interpretation of the site, which includes the house and a collection of more than 100,000 family papers, objects, and furniture. The Wyck Rose Garden dates to the 1820s, the oldest garden in the United States. The garden includes original roses from the 19th century. Several varieties thought lost were discovered growing at Wyck.

Kennywood Park ride, see entry on p. 160.

SOUTHWEST

Allegheny County Courthouse and Jail
436 Grant St., Pittsburgh; (412) 350-6500; alleghenycounty.us/ About/History/Courthouse-and-Jail.aspx; open year-round, except national holidays; guided tours on Mon; no admission charged

When the Allegheny County Courthouse was destroyed by fire in 1882, the commissioners decided to hold a design competition for the replacement. They sent letters to 100 American architects asking them to submit designs for a new courthouse. On January 31, 1884, Boston architect Henry Hobson Richardson was selected.

Few architects have a style named after their work, but the Richardsonian Romanesque style of architecture became one of the most important influences in the field, inspiring the work of other successful architects such as Louis Sullivan and Stanford White. His signature style included heavy masonry walls, hipped roofs, curved arches, and sculptural forms. The Allegheny County Courthouse is considered one of the very best examples of his style.

Construction on the courthouse and jail began in 1884. The jail was completed in 1886 and the courthouse in 1888. Romanesque architectural details include Syrian arches, a French Renaissance roof, and French Gothic dormer windows. The most impressive feature of the courthouse is the square 229-foot tower that rises high above the silhouettes of the varied roof lines, towers, and turrets. The courthouse and jail are built of large rusticated blocks of granite, and the windows are topped with wide arches. The Richardsonian Romanesque style was quite popular for municipal and public buildings, because it gave the buildings an imposing, stable, and dignified appearance.

The courthouse is a large hollow rectangle built around an interior courtyard, allowing abundant natural light and fresh air to reach the building. A noteworthy interior feature is the main staircase, which rises from the basement to the second floor in short broad flights, supported and adorned by massive limestone arches.

The jail was constructed in the shape of an irregular cross, the center of which is an octagonal tower that housed the guardrooms. It is connected to the courthouse by the Bridge of Sighs, an enclosed stone arch bridge whose design is based on the bridge of the same name in Venice, Italy. Although the courthouse is still in use, the jail, which was officially closed in 1995, has been converted into a new combined home of the juvenile and family sections of the Common Pleas Court. The Old Allegheny County Jail Museum is open Monday, staffed by docents from the Pittsburgh History & Landmarks Foundation.

Richardson did not live to see the completion of the courthouse, dying of kidney disease at the age of 47 in 1886. He considered this commission one of the high points of his career. In ill health and in his last years, he wrote, "Let me have time

to finish Pittsburgh, and I should be content without another day." This remarkable example of the Richardsonian Romanesque style designed by the architect who created the style became a National Historic Landmark in 1976.

Bost Building
**623 E. Eighth Ave., Homestead; (412) 464-4020; riversofsteel.com/
preservation/heritage-sites/bost-building; open weekdays year-
round; admission charged**

Between June 29 and November 21, 1892, much of the nation followed the events
of a labor strike in Homestead that pitted the Carnegie Steel Company against one
of the strongest labor unions at the time, the Amalgamated Association of Iron and
Steel Workers. During the strike at the Homestead Steel Works, the Bost Building,
built earlier in the year as the Columbia Hotel, served as union headquarters and the
base for newspaper correspondents reporting the events.

Andrew Carnegie, who in his speeches and writings expressed support for the
worker and the labor unions, placed his partner, Henry Clay Frick, in charge of his
companies, understanding that Frick wanted to break the union at Homestead and
elsewhere. On May 18, 1892, Carnegie announced that the contract with the union
was scheduled for renewal on June 30 and that the new terms would feature a sliding
scale based on sales and production, resulting in substantial wage reductions. All
positions in the mill would be vacated, and workers would need to reapply for work
and sign a three-year agreement that prohibited them from being a member of the
union.

On June 27 Homestead steelworkers unanimously agreed not to accept the pro-
posal. On June 29 Frick locked the workers out of the plant and began hiring strike-
breakers. The striking
workers were determined
to keep them out of the
plant, forming 24-hour
watches and barricades
to keep the town closed.
After several thwarted
attempts to get replace-
ment workers to reopen
the plant, Frick arranged
for Pinkerton guards to
approach the plant by
river barge.

On July 6 armed
Pinkerton guards arrived
on the banks of the
Monongahela River, but
the striking workers and

their families were waiting for them. The bloody confrontation became known as the Battle of Homestead. In all, nine strikers and seven Pinkertons were killed, and others on both sides were injured. The sheriff, unable to recruit residents against the strikers, appealed to the governor for militia support, which arrived on July 12. The soldiers surrounded the plant and displaced the picketers, and management regained control of the mill.

The mill reopened with replacement workers, and the strike continued. Eventually support for the union waned, and workers gradually began accepting the lower wages and returning to work. Finally, on November 21, the strike ended, and the union vacated the Bost Building. The individual workers at Homestead paid heavily for the strike. After the strike, steelworkers continued working without the protection of a union until the labor movement in the 1930s changed that.

The Bost Building, designated a National Historic Landmark in 1999, remains an important touchstone of the events of 1892. The Bost Building underwent a $4 million renovation and in 2002 opened its doors as the visitor center for the Rivers of Steel National Heritage Area. It includes an exhibit space dedicated to the American worker as well as offices for the Heritage Area.

Braddock Carnegie Library
**419 Library St., Braddock; (412) 351-5356;
braddockcarnegielibrary.org; open year-round; no admission charged**

The Braddock Carnegie Library is the first Carnegie Library in the United States. Andrew Carnegie led the expansion of the American steel industry in the late 19th century and became one of the wealthiest individuals in American history. Born in Scotland in 1835, he emigrated with his family to the Pittsburgh area in search of a better life. He attributed his success to the access he had to an extensive private collection of books. He believed that funding library construction would provide the same opportunity to everyone. He became a leading philanthropist in the United States, funding 1,689 public libraries between 1883 and 1929. During the last 18 years of his life, he gave away about $350 million to charities, foundations, and universities, almost 90 percent of his fortune.

Designed by William Halsey Wood in an eclectic medieval style, the Braddock Library was built in 1888 and dedicated by Carnegie in 1889, interestingly right after his workers agreed to a less favorable new contract. A Richardson Romanesque–style addition was constructed in 1893 by Longfellow, Alden & Harlow (successors to H. H. Richardson). In addition to the library, it included a bathhouse in the basement that workers could access via a tunnel from the factory, providing a place to shower at a time when indoor plumbing was limited. Billiards, quite fashionable at the time, could be played on the first floor. The addition doubled the size of the building and added a 964-seat music hall, a gymnasium, a swimming pool, and a two-lane duckpin alley. The library remained free, but the other amenities could be accessed only by members of the Carnegie Club. Employees of any Carnegie-owned company received a 50 percent discount, making the price $1 per quarter. Carnegie's vision for his libraries included what he termed "the three fountains," a place for the mind, the body, and the spirit.

By the mid-1960s, with its endowment gone and a badly leaking roof, the library stopped using almost all the spaces except the main library. In 1974 it closed, and by 1978 it was scheduled for demolition. An effort, led by the last librarian and local residents who formed Braddock's Field Historical Society, purchased the building for $1. It was initially reopened in 1983 on weekends only with kerosene heat and an emergency generator. Slowly, room by room, the building was rehabilitated. The wood-panel gym was completed in 1995, and the original terra-cotta roof was restored in 1999. Work on the building continues, funded by private donations and state grants.

The library, designated a National Historic Landmark in 2012, is operated by the Braddock Carnegie Library Association.

Cambria Iron Company
104 Iron St., Johnstown; (814) 539-1880; jaha.org; open year-round; guided tours by appointment; no admission charged

Founded in 1852 to supply iron rails for the nation's rapidly growing railroad network, the Cambria Iron Company grew to be America's largest ironworks by the 1870s. As it expanded during the late 19th century, Cambria attracted leading engineers, innovators, and managers to Johnstown, and the city became a leader in technological innovations in the iron and steel industry.

Industrial designs that were developed here were widely copied by other iron and steel companies throughout the country. These contributions included experimentation with the Kelly converter, early conversion to the Bessemer steel process in 1871,

and the first US commercial producer of steel railroad rails in 1867. The company became the Cambria Steel Company in 1898. Bethlehem Steel Company purchased the company in 1923, and under the stewardship of the country's second-largest steel company, it continued to expand. The plant's history reflects the nationwide evolution of the iron and steel industry.

When the Bethlehem Steel Company filed for bankruptcy in 2003, the Johnstown Redevelopment Authority was able to purchase 10 acres and three key structures (the blacksmith shop, the machine shop, and the carpenter shop). Originally built in 1863, the blacksmith shop is the most historically significant of the remaining structures. The brick structure has an octagonal shape with an octagonal cupola built with heavy-timbered roof trusses and iron tension rods. It was enlarged in 1870 and again in 1885. Original turn-of-the-20th-century forging tools remain, including a variety of steam-powered hammers. A 10-ton steam hammer owned by the Smithsonian Institute remains in place and is leased to the Redevelopment Authority. The 200 workers in the blacksmith shop were capable of doing all the repairs to the equipment throughout the plant.

The Center for Metal Arts, a nonprofit school and a national leader in metalworking and blacksmithing, is using the blacksmith shop as their classroom, utilizing some of the old equipment including the industrial hammers. The Cambria Iron Company was designated a National Historic Landmark in 1989. The Cambria Iron Works site is connected by a pedestrian trail to the Johnstown central business district and the Cambria City National Historic District.

Carrie Blast Furnaces, Numbers 6 and 7
Carrie Furnace Blvd., Rankin; (412) 464-4020; riversofsteel.com/
preservation/heritage-sites/carrie-furnaces; tours offered May
through Oct; admission charged

Built in 1907, Carrie Furnaces 6 and 7 produced iron for the Homestead Iron Works
until 1978. Situated along the Monongahela River, the furnaces rise 92 feet in height
and are rare examples of pre–World War II iron making technology. The Carrie
Blast Furnace Plant served two functions. Primarily it produced basic iron for the
steelwork's open-hearth furnaces. It also produced by-product gas that was utilized
to generate electrical power. In many areas of the Monongahela Valley, power plants
operating on blast furnace gas generated enough excess electricity to serve all the
needs of the industrial facility and the surrounding communities. Blast furnaces
were defining elements in the steel town landscape and were as interwoven into the
communities as any ethnic church or social hall.

As their name implies, Carrie 6 and 7 were the sixth and seventh furnaces constructed at the site. The increased output helped US Steel increase its annual iron-
making capacity from about 980,000 tons in 1912 to over 2 million tons by the end
of World War II. At that time Carrie 6 and 7 were each producing between 900 and
1,000 tons of iron a day.

The molten iron produced at Carrie was transported across the river on the Hot Metal Bridge to the Homestead Steel Works, where it was transformed into steel. The bridge, built in 1901 by the Keystone Bridge Works, was part of the expansion of the Carrie plant that included the construction of furnaces 3 and 4. The bridge was composed of a massive Pennsylvania through-truss main span and a smaller Baltimore through-truss span. Because of the tremendous load it had to support, the bridge was constructed with extremely heavy structural members and the heaviest span built at the time. The bridge carried two rail tracks and a sidewalk. The upstream track transported raw materials, and the downstream (hot metal side) carried ladle cars filled with molten iron. The bridge provided the only direct link for hot metal transport between the Carrie furnaces and the Homestead Steel Works from 1901 until the facility closed in 1978.

Although much of the Homestead site was demolished after its closure, the two blast furnaces remained and became the stage for a unique example of industrial salvage artwork. In 1997 Guerilla artists, sneaking into the site over the course of a year, created a 40-foot deer using materials salvaged entirely from the site. Since the sculpture was created as a momentary, site-specific art event, there was little thought given to its permanence. Fifteen years later, it was balanced precariously on a deteriorating building that began to collapse, causing the deer to tilt. Arts activists and historic preservationists organized a "Save the Deer" movement that included a funding campaign and a documentary in 2014, ensuring its preservation.

The site is owned by the Rivers of Steel National Heritage Area and is being preserved and interpreted. It was designated a National Historic Landmark in 2006.

David Bradford House
175 S. Main St., Washington; (724) 222-3604; bradfordhouse.org; tours available year-round by appointment; admission charged

Constructed in 1788, this two-and-one-half-story stone house was the residence of lawyer David Bradford. He grew quite wealthy from his practice, and his house reflected that wealth with fine interiors and beautiful furnishings. As one of the leading politicians in the area, Bradford was drawn into the controversy that led to the famous Whiskey Rebellion of 1794.

The American Revolution was a financial disaster for most individual states, and by the end of the war, most had large amounts of debt. Treasury Secretary Alexander Hamilton worked to persuade the federal government to assume that debt in 1790. One solution he offered was to impose an excise tax on whiskey. Although President George Washington opposed the whiskey tax, Congress passed the bill.

Even though local officials had encouraged the passage of the tax, local protests immediately began asserting that the tax was unfair to smaller producers. The law set rates on the amount of whiskey that could be produced. Larger producers paid an annual rate of 6 cents per gallon, while smaller producers paid 9 cents per gallon.

By 1794 the uprising of farmers and distillers in Western Pennsylvania was escalating. Excise officers sent to collect the taxes were met with violence, some even tarred and feathered. As violence increased, locals were warned that Washington would send militia to deal with the responsible individuals. Bradford, along with several other men, attacked a mail carrier and discovered three letters from Pittsburgh expressing disapproval over the local violence against the tax collectors. Bradford, envisioning himself a new George Washington, organized a march on Pittsburgh with 7,000 men. To avoid violence, the City of Pittsburgh sent word that the three letter writers had been ousted from the city. They offered a gift of several barrels of whiskey to appease the protesters. The day ended with the rebels drunk from the whiskey and no longer inspired to descend on Pittsburgh.

The issue with the tax, however, was not resolved, and after a peaceful envoy failed, Washington led 12,000 state militia from Pennsylvania and the surrounding

states to Western Pennsylvania. It was the first and last time a sitting president led armed troops. The militia was met with angry citizens but little violence. Washington rounded up suspected rebels who were sent to Philadelphia to stand trial. Upon learning that he would be arrested, Bradford fled south to Spanish West Florida (now Louisiana). He took up a new life there with his family. Eventually Bradford received a pardon for his role in the Whiskey Rebellion.

In 1959 the Pennsylvania Historical and Museum Commission assumed control of the David Bradford House and supervised a complete restoration. It is owned and operated by the Bradford Historical Association as a house museum and is furnished in period pieces from the time the house was constructed. It was designated a National Historic Landmark in 1983.

Edward G. Acheson House

908 W. Main St., Monongahela; (724) 292-8247; monongahelahistoricalsociety.com; private residence not open to the public; downloadable walking tour of area featuring house available on website

Edward Goodrich Acheson, a native of nearby Washington, Pennsylvania, purchased this house in 1890. Beginning his life with little education, he worked several jobs before deciding his dream was to be an inventor. Fascinated by the latest developments in electricity, he moved to New York. He had the good fortune to meet Thomas Edison, who gave him a job in Menlo Park. He demonstrated his mechanical talents and was sent to Paris in 1881 to help set up a lamp exhibition at the Paris Exposition. In 1885 Acheson returned to Pennsylvania to start his own laboratory. In 1890 he moved to Monongahela to build an electric system of street lighting for the town. At night he sold his electricity to the town, and during the day he used it for his experiments.

Although he lived in this simple Victorian-era house for only five years, it was the most important time of his life. Using the summer kitchen he had converted to his laboratory, Acheson's experiments led to the invention of Carborundum, or silicon carbide, for which he received a patent in 1893. Carborundum is a mixture of clay and powdered coke, fused by electric current. Carborundum was, and for 50 years remained, the hardest artificial substance in the world. It was used in many industrial processes, primarily as an abrasive. Acheson established a manufacturing plant for Carborundum in Monon-

gahela, but demand for the product soon exceeded the capacity of the plant, and he relocated to Niagara Falls, New York.

Acheson continued his work in Niagara Falls, discovering that overheating Carborundum produces almost pure graphite, and further learning that the silicon vaporizes and leaves behind graphitic carbon, a very effective lubricant. He received a patent for that product in 1896. The Acheson Graphite Company was formed in 1899. Acheson received recognition for the invention of Carborundum, earning the John Scott Medal by the Franklin Institute in 1894. He received the prize a second time in 1901 for his invention of artificial graphite. His company merged with National Carbon Company in 1928 (now Union Carbide).

A man from humble beginnings, Acheson was fascinated with science, and he used that interest to become a leader in the field of abrasives and lubricants for manufacturing. His house in Monongahela was the base of his rise to success, a success that is even more remarkable given his lack of a formal education and that he worked independently from his home laboratory. His home in Monongahela earned National Historic Landmark status in 1976. The house is in private ownership but is featured on walking tours by the Monongahela Area Historical Society, including a very popular annual Candlelight Ghost Walk.

Emmanuel Episcopal Church
957 W. North Ave., Pittsburgh; (412) 231-0454; emmanuelpgh.org; contact for tour; no admission charged

Architect Henry Hobson Richardson is credited with the design of many well-known buildings, including Trinity Church in Boston and the Allegheny County Courthouse and Jail in Pittsburgh (see related entry). However, the small and less elaborate Emmanuel Episcopal Church is one of his best and most interesting designs.

Emmanuel Episcopal Church began as a mission in 1867 by a group of ladies in Allegheny, located across the river from Pittsburgh, who felt there was a need for a Sunday school. In the beginning Emmanuel Mission, as it was called, met in homes and then in rented rooms. The pupils were primarily the children of English workmen at the local factories in Manchester, now Northside. In 1868 the group received a charter to incorporate Emmanuel Episcopal Church. A frame church building was constructed in 1869.

A building committee was formed in 1882 to address the need for a larger building. The congregation was young, prosperous, and growing. They wanted something that was new and different, something designed in a progressive style like the work of Richardson. The first design called for a quarry-faced ashlar church, but the design was rejected as being too expensive. The final bid, based on the revised design, was

$12,000, half the cost of the original. It utilized brick, a less expensive building material, and eliminated the tower and all the sculpture.

The building is a one-story simple rectangle with a semicircular apse, a projection containing the altar. The walls are red brick with delicate brick patterning and detailing. The wall surfaces are mostly plain, although the bricks do project from the main wall surface just below the eaves in two steps, producing a string course. The roof is a steep gable with the ridge running north and south. It is slate covered with a molded copper ridge cap. The steep roof descends to relatively low sidewalls. Inside the sanctuary the handsome wood-paneled ceiling is supported by the exposed wood-truss system. The use of dark wood and strong lines contrast with the white marble reredos (large decorative screens) and the white marble and mosaic tiles of the chancel.

Completed in 1886, the church is known for its architectural features and was one of the last designs by Richardson, who died the same year at age 46. It was designated a National Historic Landmark in 2000.

F. Julius LeMoyne House
49 E. Maiden St., Washington; (724) 225-6740; wchspa.org/leymoynehouse; tours available year-round, Tues through Fri; admission charged

Built in 1812 by John LeMoyne, the father of Francis Julius LeMoyne (known as Julius), the seven-bay-wide stone Georgian house with Greek Revival styling served as both the home and medical office for Dr. John LeMoyne and eventually his son (Julius) as well. Traditionally, Georgian style houses have a center entrance flanked by an equal number of windows on either side. In this case a second, less prominent entrance led to the office and apothecary.

After graduating from Washington College, Julius apprenticed in the medical practice, then studied medicine at Jefferson Medical College in Philadelphia. In 1823 he married Madelaine Bureau. Shortly after his marriage, Julius's father suffered bankruptcy. Julius prevented the foreclosure on his father's property by borrowing money to purchase the family home and farms and then worked to clear his father's debts. His father moved out of the family house in 1827, and Julius lived there until his death in 1879.

Julius LeMoyne joined the antislavery crusade just as it was becoming a national movement. In 1834 a local group seeking to organize a new society in Washington County persuaded Julius to join the Washington County Anti-Slavery Society. He served as its president from 1835 until 1837. Julius, his wife, and older daughters became heavily involved, making their house a center of antislavery activities. He worked with other abolitionists to sponsor rallies and bring in speakers. When he

was recruited by the American Anti-Slavery Society in 1837 to be their agent, he expanded his activities beyond the county. The house became a depot for antislavery literature, which was distributed throughout the Ohio Valley. Julius communicated with antislavery groups across the country.

The Underground Railroad was active in Washington County by the time Julius joined the antislavery cause. By about 1815 a system of trails for runaway slaves was emerging in Southwestern Pennsylvania. By the 1830s it was an operational network that stayed active through the Civil War between Eastern Pennsylvania and Ohio. Despite the strict Fugitive Slave Law of 1850, Julius risked his personal freedom and made his home a safe station for fugitives. His correspondence from the 1840s includes several letters from individuals who asked for aid or thanked him for his assistance in getting them or their relatives out of the South.

In 1879 Julius's will divided the property into thirds, leaving lots to his daughter Ann and son Frank, and the house and its lot to his daughters Jane and Madeleine. Madeleine willed the house and the front half of the lot to the Washington County Historical Society. It now serves as the headquarters and museum of the Washington County Historical Society. It was designated a National Historic Landmark in 1997.

Fallingwater
1491 Mill Run Rd., Mill Run; (724) 329-8501; fallingwater.org; open year-round; admission charged

Frank Lloyd Wright designed a summer home for Pittsburgh department store owner Edgar J. Kaufmann that is recognized as one of the most important 20th-century houses in the United States. The partnership between Kaufmann and Wright began when Edgar Kaufmann Jr. studied with Wright at his studio, Taliesin. Wright's first commission with Kaufmann was to design his corner office on the 10th floor of Kaufmann's Department Store. In 1934 Wright visited Bear Run and began work on what would be known as Fallingwater.

The Kaufmanns' love for Bear Run's rushing waterfalls inspired their architect to imagine a residence cantilevered over the falls. While the Kaufmanns expected their home to be situated with a view of the falls, Wright imagined something more organic. He positioned a massive central stone chimney above the falls and created a series of stacked concrete levels that appear to float above the water with no visible support.

The structure of the main house is sandstone, with floors of cantilevered slabs of reinforced concrete. Millwork is black walnut. Wright built in furniture and used fluorescent lighting as an aesthetic element, which imitates daylight or is used as indirect light. Structural materials are generally the same on both interior and exterior, the flagstone-paved living room floor opens to a stair leading down to a plunge

pool. The windows at the corners have no visible supports, so there is no visual interruption of the view outside. The equal importance of indoor and outdoor spaces is evidenced by almost equal square footage of the inside rooms and outside terraces.

The first story contains a large central living room, with a dining table and glazed hatch leading down steps to the stream. The kitchen and entry are surprisingly small. The house is surrounded by terraces that emphasize easy access from interior to exterior spaces on all levels. From the living room the terraces on the east and west are accessed through steel and glass doors. The master bedroom and terrace are on the second story above the living room. Mr. Kaufmann's dressing room is located above the kitchen and opens onto a terrace. A guest bedroom is also located above the east side of the living room. The third story includes a "gallery" that opens onto a terrace above the center of the house, a bedroom located above the dressing room, and a set of stairs that terminates on the west terrace.

Construction of Fallingwater was completed in 1937, and the Kaufmann family began using their weekend retreat and sharing it with family and friends. Fallingwater's popularity necessitated that a guest house be built in 1939, connected to the main house by a cascading concrete canopy. In 1963 Edgar Kaufmann Jr., presented the house, contents, and grounds to the Western Pennsylvania Conservancy. The ongoing tasks of maintenance and preservation of Fallingwater began shortly after its completion and included a major restoration in 2001 and 2002. The Western Pennsylvania Conservancy has been an excellent steward of this masterpiece, undertaking major and minor carefully planned preservation projects since accepting the property and continually monitoring its condition to ensure its preservation into the future. It was designated a National Historic Landmark in 1976. The house is open to the public.

I. N. & Bernadine Hagen House (Kentuck Knob)
723 Kentuck Rd., Chalk Hill; (724) 329-1901; kentuckknob .com; open daily Mar through Oct, hours vary in winter; admission charged

The Hagen House is a nationally significant work of American architect Frank Lloyd Wright, who designed many houses during his career. While most Usonian houses were standardized and simplified to appeal to a larger market, Kentuck Knob is one of just a few examples of a high-end, customized Usonian design, and it represented a change in Wright's ideas for a house. It was no longer assumed that every homeowner would employ domestic help. Instead, Wright envisioned the owners maintaining the house themselves. The interiors were less formal, using an open floor plan that served several functions.

Isaac Newton (I. N.) and Bernadine Hagen were the owners of the Hagen Ice Cream Company in Uniontown. They met Wright in the early 1950s through mutual

friends, the Edgar Kaufmann family, owners of Fallingwater (see related entry). The Hagens met with Wright in 1953 to discuss their interest in a new house, much less elaborate than Fallingwater, but with the same organic feeling. Wright's concept of a Usonian home embraced his ideas of organic architecture, a concept that nature be included in every aspect of the home. The home was to appear to have come up from the ground into the fresh air and sunshine.

In siting the house, Wright did not select the top of the knob, which would have provided commanding views of the Youghiogheny River Gorge. Instead he selected a more challenging site immediately south of the knob. The house is nestled into the side of the knob, allowing the building to appear organic and harmonious with the landscape rather than dominating it. Wright was always concerned about natural light, so he oriented the house to the south and west so that it would always have the best light year-round. Constructed of native stone, tidewater cypress, and copper, the crescent-shaped house curls around a west-facing courtyard. The anchor of the design is a hexagonal stone core that rises from the hipped roof at the intersection of the living and bedroom wings. The flat-roofed carport and studio walls are buried within the knob of the hill and create the courtyard's eastern side.

The Hagens moved from Uniontown into Kentuck Knob in July 1956 on their 26th wedding anniversary and spent the next 30 years there. "There is a sense of beauty, comfort, serenity and harmony in the house and all of its surroundings," said Mrs. Hagan. The Hagans resided in the house until the early 1980s. After I. N. fell ill, the Hagans could no longer remain on the mountain, so they sold the

home in 1986 to Lord Peter Palumbo of London, England, who has continued to maintain the beauty and tradition of the house. In 1996 Palumbo opened the house to the public. The house was designated a National Historic Landmark in 2000. The woodlands and grounds at Kentuck Knob offer the perfect setting for a remarkable sculpture collection by modern artists such as Andy Goldsworthy, Sir Anthony Caro, Wendy Taylor, and Phillip King. The owner's collection of 30 sculptures can be viewed along the Woodland Walking Trail that connects the house to the visitor center.

Kennywood Park
4800 Kennywood Blvd., West Mifflin; (412) 461-0500; kennywood .com; open daily Memorial Day through Labor Day; admission charged

Open to the public in 1898 as a small trolley park near Pittsburgh, Kennywood was created by the Monongahela Street Railway Company in an era when these companies created amusement parks away from the city. This increased the usage of the trolley on the weekends and provided recreation away from the heat and crowds. The development of Kennywood Park documents the growth and trends in the amusement industry in America, as well as the technological advances and innovations that contribute to its success. Buildings, structures, or rides from nearly every era of its

history are preserved while the park continues to update its attractions to remain a popular destination.

Kennywood still contains two major buildings that date to the 19th century: a carousel pavilion that has been converted to a restaurant and the casino (a social gathering place at the time), now the Parkside Café. The 1898 paddle boats are still a popular attraction. In 1901 the Old Mill opened, and although it has been modified, it is the world's oldest continuously operating dark water ride. The Whip dates to 1918 and is still in use. In 1927 "Kenny's Karousel" was installed and featured four rows of beautiful hand-carved figures, including 64 horses (50 that moved up and down and 14 that were stationary), 1 lion, 1 tiger, and 4 chariots. The carousel was completely refurbished in 1975 and 1976. Each animal was stripped, sanded, and repainted to its original coloring by art students from Carnegie-Mellon University. The present carousel shelter building dates to 1927 and was constructed to house this carousel. Noah's Ark, built in 1936, is a walk-through funhouse that remains one of the park's most famous symbols.

Of the 17 roller coasters built at Kennywood between 1902 and the present, 7 are still operating, including the 1921 Jack Rabbit, the 1927 Racer, and the 1968 Thunderbolt. The Jack Rabbit was the first Kennywood coaster to use the under-friction wheel system, enabling higher speeds, higher hills, and a more thrilling ride than had been possible before. Kennywood has been called the "Roller Coaster Capital of the World," and three of its coasters, the Jack Rabbit, the Racer, and the Pippin

(1924), later converted to the Thunderbolt, have been named Landmark Rides by the American Coaster Enthusiasts. Kennywood Park was designated a National Historic Landmark in 1987.

In 1996 Lost Kennywood opened as a themed area presenting rides and architecture of the past. For more than 100 years, Kennywood was owned and operated locally. Since 2007 it has been owned by Spanish-based Parques Reundios, one of the largest amusement park operators in the world.

Meadowcroft Rockshelter
401 Meadowcroft Rd., Avella; (724) 587-3412; heinzhistorycenter .org/meadowcroft; open weekends, May through Oct, and additional hours in summer; admission charged

In 1955 Albert Miller discovered what looked to be a prehistoric tool near a groundhog hole on his family's farm. Miller, an amateur archaeologist, understood that he had potentially found something very important that should be investigated further. It took him 18 years to find a professional who would undertake the work. Dr. James Adovasio, from the University of Pittsburgh, conducted the first field school there in 1973. Astonished by the artifact, which was a prehistoric flint knife, a team of archaeology, anthropology, and geology students studied the area as part of a curriculum. The excavation of the site over the next six years yielded nearly 2 million

objects including ancient stone tools, pottery fragments, animal and plant remains, and evidence of ice-age fire pits.

Meadowcroft Rockshelter features a massive rock overhang that was used for shelter 16,000 years ago, the oldest site of human habitation in North America. An award-winning, visitor-friendly enclosure, completed in 2008, allows for the protection of the site while providing the optimum view of the ongoing archaeological excavation. Prehistoric occupations of Meadowcroft Rockshelter can be assigned to the Paleo-Indian (pre-10,000 B.P.), Archaic (10,000 to 3,000 B.P.), Woodland (3,000 to 450 B.P.) and Historic Periods (450 B.P. to present).

Meadowcroft Rockshelter is one of the most important sites excavated in the eastern United States, because no other site in the United States has provided such a well-dated sequence of cultural occupation at one location. In the center of the site lies the partially excavated remains of a fire pit that dates to the end of the last ice age. The excavation uncovered 1.4 million plant remains, providing information on what was growing here over the past 16,000 years; almost 1 million animal remains; and over 20,000 artifacts. One of the most important artifacts is the Miller Lance-olate Point, a discovery that suggested that the continent was inhabited more than 11,500 years earlier than previously documented. Making Meadowcroft Rockshelter accessible to visitors, a practice that is not typical of sensitive archaeological sites, has resulted in the general public becoming interested in archaeology and the migration

of the United States. It is a connection between the professional practice of archaeology and the public.

Meadowcroft is also the site of a series of interpretive villages that demonstrates rural life over the past 500 years, including a 16th-century Eastern Woodland Indian Village, an 18th-century log cabin and open-sided trading post, and a 19th-century village that includes a church, one-room schoolhouse, and blacksmith shop. A rehabilitated covered bridge provides access to the village. The 1871 Pine Bank Covered Bridge is one of only about 20 remaining examples of a kingpost-truss bridge in the United States.

Meadowcroft Rockshelter and Historic Village is owned and operated by the John Heinz History Center. The site was designated a National Historic Landmark in 2005.

Oakmont Country Club
1233 Hulton Rd., Oakmont; (412) 828-8000; oakmont-countryclub .org; free guided tours on Mon with advance reservation

In 1903, 100 men and 25 horse teams transformed a pasture into a golf course to closely resemble the barren courses of Scotland, the birthplace of golf. The native oaks were removed and a "parkland" course, 6,600 yards in length, was created with narrow fairways and large greens. This challenging course with areas of rough and as many as 300 sand bunkers was considered one of the most difficult in the world.

Now lengthened to 6,989 yards but with its original layout virtually intact, the course is still considered one of the most difficult in North America. The greens are large, hard (built on a gravel and clay base), sloped, and closely cut, making them extremely fast. Fairways were so narrow that they have been widened at the request of the US Golf Association for championship events. Sand bunkers are still the primary hazard, a few of them renowned for their size and difficulty. The Church Pews Bunker contains 12 berms, each covered in thick, shaggy fescue (tufted grass). The bunker is 4 feet deep in many places, and each of the berms is 3 feet high, with 5 yards of sand between each one. The bunker is more than 100 yards long, 43 yards across at its widest point, and 18 yards across at its narrowest.

The course, which sits high above the Allegheny River, was designed by Henry C. Fownes, who founded the club in 1903. An accomplished amateur designer, Fownes's son William continued to make changes to the course for many years. Several famous golf course architects have done restoration and renovation work at Oakmont through the years, including Robert Trent Jones Sr., Arnold Palmer and Ed Seay, and Arthur Hills. The most recent work was completed in 2006 by golf course architect Tom Fazio. Oakmont Country Club, with its well-known challenging course, has hosted more USGA and PGA championships than any other course in the United States. It served as the host to nine US Opens, five US Amateurs, three PGA Championships, and two US Women's Opens.

The 1904 Tudor Revival–style clubhouse, with broad porches and its elegant interior, has been carefully preserved. The clubhouse is filled with historic photos of the building, the course, notable tournaments, and famous golfers who played there. The Oakmont Country Club was designated a National Historic Landmark in 1987. Although it is a private club, regular tours are offered by Pittsburgh History and Landmarks.

Old Economy
**270 Sixteenth St., Ambridge; (724) 266-4500; oldeconomyvillage
.org; open Apr through Dec; admission charged**

The Harmonists left Germany in 1804 seeking religious freedom. Under the leadership of George Rapp and his adopted son Frederick, they established their first settlement, named Harmony, in Butler County. In 1814 they moved to Indiana and established New Harmony, before returning to Pennsylvania in 1824. They established their third and final community on 3,000 acres along the Ohio River in Beaver County. Economy was one of the most successful of 19th-century American utopian communities, and the Harmony Society achieved national recognition for its wool, cotton, and silk industries and its pioneering role in the oil industry and the construction of several railroads. Economy was a model for other utopian groups of the period such as the Shakers, the Amana Society, and the Zoarites.

Based on the teachings of the early Christian Church, the Harmonists lived a simple, pietistic life. Members turned over everything they owned to the Harmony Society when they joined. The entire society worked together for the good of all

in exchange for receiving only what they needed to live comfortably and simply. In 1807, in anticipation of Christ's Second Coming that they believed would occur very soon, they became celibate in order to purify themselves. They wanted to be ready for Christ's 1,000-year reign on Earth.

One of the longest-lived of the many utopian communities, the Harmony Society was eventually weakened by the death of its founders, George in 1834 and Frederick in 1847. Splits within the group and a diminishing population led to its dissolution in 1905, 100 years after its founding. In 1916 the Commonwealth of Pennsylvania acquired 6 acres and 17 buildings of Old Economy to preserve as a historic site. It was the first property purchased by the state for historic purposes and eventually became one of 29 historic sites owned by the Commonwealth. Other parts of the society's lands and buildings were acquired by the American Bridge Company to expand the borough of Ambridge.

Old Economy Village, designated a National Historic Landmark in 1965, is maintained by the Pennsylvania Historical and Museum Commission and operated by the Friends of Old Economy Village, a nonprofit community organization.

Searights Tollhouse
7328 National Pike East, Uniontown; (724) 439-4422; fayettehistoricalsociety.org; open Sat and Sun year-round; no admission charged

Presidents Washington and Jefferson both believed that a road that crossed the Appalachian Mountains was needed to expand and unify the new United States of America. In 1806 Congress authorized the construction of the National Road (originally called the Cumberland Road) that connected the Potomac River to the Ohio River. This was the first federally funded road in the United States. Beginning in 1811 the road was completed to Cumberland, Maryland, and Uniontown, Pennsylvania, by 1817. It reached the Ohio River at Wheeling, West Virginia, by 1818. Eventually the road continued through Ohio and Indiana and terminated in Vandalia, Illinois, in the 1830s. The National Road became a major route for the transportation of goods and services. The Pennsylvania towns of Uniontown, Brownsville, and Washington became commercial centers of business and industry. Three major stagecoach lines operated in Uniontown, and Brownsville was the center for steamboat building and river freight hauling.

Heavy traffic and no maintenance caused the road to deteriorate. It was refurbished in the 1930s using the Macadam System. Developed by Scotsman John MacAdam, this system consisted of a level surface raised above the ground to allow for drainage and a series of layers of crushed stone that was compacted by the traffic, creating a strong surface. This was the first use of macadam in the United States. With

the road in good condition and recognizing that the maintenance of road would be an ongoing concern, the federal government transferred ownership to the individual states.

In order to maintain the road, the states built a series of tollhouses every 15 miles. Six were built in Pennsylvania, including the Searights Tollhouse (Gate Number 3), just west of Uniontown. Built in 1835 it was named after William Searight, a Fayette County resident, tavern owner, and commissioner of the National Road in Pennsylvania. Constructed of brick with a large wraparound porch, the two-story octagonal tower is the most prominent feature. Tollhouses were built with a room above the main floor for use as a bedroom. From within the house, the toll keeper had an excellent view of the road in both directions. There was an iron gate that could be swung across the road to stop vehicles from passing until the toll had been paid.

Tolls continued to be paid until 1905. By that time both the road and the tollhouse had deteriorated. The Commonwealth of Pennsylvania undertook the restoration of the building in 1966. It is now owned by Fayette County and is operated by the Fayette County Historical Society. It was designated a National Historic Landmark in 1964 and is an important landmark along the National Road Heritage Corridor. It is one of only two remaining National Road tollhouses in Pennsylvania.

Smithfield Street Bridge
Smithfield St. over the Monongahela River, Pittsburgh; (412) 350-
4005; alleghenycounty.us; open year-round; pedestrian and vehicular
access; no admission charged

The Smithfield Street Bridge was constructed between 1881 and 1883 and designed
by Gustav Lindenthal, a young engineer from Germany who became one of America's foremost civil engineers of the 20th century. It was built as a two-span lentic-
ular truss, also called the parabolic truss because the curves of the top and bottom
chords approximate the shape of a parabola. It was Lindenthal's first great work. He
designed three other bridges in Pittsburgh and the Hell Gate Bridge in New York
City in 1914, among others. His love of art showed in his work, as his bridges were
well designed and aesthetically pleasing.

In 1890 and 1891 a third two-span truss doubled the bridge's width and allowed
the separation of vehicular traffic from the streetcar lines, a modification that was
included in the original plans. This third span was moved 4.5 feet upstream to provide wider access in 1911. The steel trusses are supported by rusticated stone piers
with wrought-iron portal archways on the two end piers.

Between 1911 and 1915 the original wrought iron portals were removed and
replaced with new cast steel ones that are still in place. The portals are designed
in the Norman Romanesque style with elliptical basket-handle arches, a crenelated

cornice, and a trifoil arch band under the cornice with heraldic plaques. Larger plaques are positioned at the crown of the arches. The columns are topped with spires supporting spiked spheres.

The Smithfield Street Bridge is an important structure in the history of American engineering. One of the first steel trusses in the United States, it became a symbolic landmark for the American steel industry. It is a National Historic Civic Engineering Landmark and was designated a National Historic Landmark in 1976.

In the early 1990s the Pennsylvania Department of Transportation planned to demolish the bridge and replace it. Local historians lobbied for its preservation, and in 1994 and 1995 it was rehabilitated with a new deck, a colorful paint scheme, and architectural lighting. The bridge remains in use with four vehicular lanes and two pedestrian lanes. It is the most heavily walked pedestrian bridge in Pittsburgh, connecting downtown with Station Square.

Staple Bend Tunnel
1189 Beech Hill Rd., Johnstown; (814) 886-6150; nps.gov/alpo; open year-round; no admission charged

Built as part of the Allegheny Portage Railroad (see related entry), the Staple Bend Tunnel was advertised as the first railroad tunnel in the United States. It was the third tunnel built in the country; the first two were for canals in Pennsylvania. Work

on the tunnel began in November 1831. The men were paid $13 per month plus room and board and worked 12-hour days 6 days a week. Workers blasted through 901 feet of solid rock, working from both ends of the tunnel simultaneously.

This was done by drilling 3-foot-long holes and packing them with powder. Drilling one typical hole took up to three hours of hard effort using a three-man crew. Nine to 10 holes, each 1 inch in diameter and 36 inches in length, were made before blasting. The process to blast the tunnel included wrapping one pound of explosive powder in paper and inserting it into each hole. It was tamped down and punctured with a needle and then a fuse was inserted. Explosions were timed to occur during mealtimes so that the dust could settle while the workers were on break. The workers would return to the job and begin cleaning out the debris. The tunnel grew about 18 inches each day, with each crew working toward the center. On December 21, 1832, the center was reached, and both sides were connected. The tunnel excavation was completed in 1833.

The entrance portals are classically designed with paired Doric pilasters and a monumental entablature across the top. The tunnel entrances feature square cut stones surrounding the arch. This design was meant to impress railroad travelers and the general public, and nearly half of the cost of the tunnel was spent on the entrances. Sometime after the Portage Railroad ceased operations, the eastern portal was partially disassembled. The western portal was retained and has been restored to its original appearance.

The tunnel was designated a National Historic Landmark in 1994. The Staple Bend Tunnel has been open as a separate area of the Allegheny Portage Railroad National Historic Site owned and operated by the National Park Service since 2001. It is not in the immediate area of the visitor center. Rather it is near the town of Mineral Point, 5 miles from Johnstown. From the trail head and parking area, it is a 2-mile walk to the Staple Bend Tunnel.

W. A. Young & Sons Foundry and Machine Shop
116 Water St., Rices Landing; (412) 464-4020; riversofsteel.com/ preservation/heritage-sites; open Sun during the summer or by appointment; admission charged

William A. Young purchased two plots of land in Rices Landing in Greene County and built a two-story machine shop. The shop is a complex of three interconnected wood-frame structures, utilitarian in appearance, with gabled roofs and clapboarded exterior. The front shop, built in 1902, houses the main machine shop on the ground floor and the pattern shop on the second floor. Attached to the rear of this building are two smaller shops, one housing the foundry, built in 1908.

Young's talent as a master carpenter enabled him to study a sketch provided by a client and make the pattern very quickly. The finished product could be ready for pick up as early as the next day.

During its operation William and his two sons manned the shop, except during World War II when the workforce increased to 30 and included women. The skills of an apprentice were tested by requiring him to build his own set of tools and toolbox before he could move from apprentice to employee. The foundry produced a variety of products, rather than focusing on a single type. Anything that could be cast in molten metal in the coke-fired furnace could be made for a client or for sale. The furnace is still extant in the building; a pile of unburned coke remains beside it. The shop produced bronze castings, pipe fittings, and locomotive wheels. It was so versatile in the type of products it could fabricate that it made items as small as a mouse trap and as large as a gear that was part of a river lock that still hangs on the wall.

A "jobbing shop" like W. A. Young and Sons was a firm that did any work that came its way, large or small. It made products for customers that included local residents and area businesses as well as large regional manufacturers, making specialized parts and performing custom jobs. As was common during this era, one system of belts and pulleys operated 25 pieces of equipment throughout the shop. Each one could operate independently with the entire system powered by one motor. Originally a 12-horsepower steam engine operated the system, replaced by a 20-horsepower electric engine, and eventually powered by a 20-horsepower gasoline engine. All the equipment dates from 1870 to 1920 and remains in place. Small shops like this were an important component in the American industrial economy.

Throughout its existence, the shop employed only a few workers that included foundrymen to operate the cupola furnace and make castings. When the last

foundryman left in the early 1930s, Young did not replace him and closed the foundry. It was not cost-effective to compete with the large-scale foundries in Pittsburgh.

The machine shop remained in operation until 1965, operated after Young's death in 1940 by his two sons. The building and its entire set of tools, patterns, and records were acquired by the Greene County Historical Society in 1985. It sold the property in 2009 to the Rivers of Steel Heritage Corporation, which has undertaken preservation of the site. The W. A. Young and Sons Foundry and Machine Shop was designated a National Historic Landmark in 2016.

Thematic Index

Photo Credits

Mindy Gulden Crawford viii, 1, 6, 9, 13, 20, 23, 64, 68, 70, 84, 90, 91, 111, 116, 126, 127 (top and bottom), 135, 136, 137, 138, 149, 154, 157, 169; Courtesy of Eastern State Penitentiary Historic Site, Inc. ix, 53; Wikimedia Commons/By Beyond My Ken - Own Work, CC BY-SA 4.0 x, 3, 32; Melissa L. Mann (courtesy of the Pennsylvania Historical and Museum Commission) 4; Wikimedia Commons/By Chris Light - Own Work, CC BY-SA 4.0 7; Wikimedia Commons/By Ron Shawley, CC BY 3.0 8; Julia D. Chain 11, 112, 113, 114; Courtesy of Preservation Pennsylvania 12, 88, 170; Lee Rainey 15 (top and bottom); Timothy E. Pavlic II 16, 17; Public Domain 18 (top), 83, 93 (top and bottom), 153, 171, 173; Wikimedia Commons/By Jeremy Thompson from United States of America - Lakemont 057Uploaded by Crazypaco, CC BY 2.0 18 (bottom); Emily Cooperman 22, 26, 36; Bonnie J. Halda 25, 28, 33, 37, 42, 48, 55, 56, 59, 61, 80, 85, 94, 96, 99, 105, 109, 110, 115, 117, 118, 120, 121, 125, 128; Sabra Smith 29, 31, 62, 63, 69, 103, 109, 130, 131; Wikimedia Commons/By Self - Own Work, CC BY 3.0 35; Courtesy of the Pennsylvania Historical and Museum Commission 39, 49; zrfphoto/Getty Images 40; Wikimedia Commons/By Pbjamesphoto - Own Work, CC BY-SA 4.0 41; Littleny/Getty Images 43; Joseph Elliot 44, 45; Courtesy of Cliveden, a Historic Site of the National Trust for Historic Preservation 46; Craig A. Benner (courtesy of the Pennsylvania Historical and Museum Commission) 51 (top and bottom); Elizabeth Bertheaud (courtesy of the Pennsylvania Historical and Museum Commission) 58; Wikimedia Commons/By Michael E. Reali Jr. (Wiki Takes Philadelphia 2 participant) - Uploaded from Wiki Takes Philadelphia 2, CC BY 3.0 66; Courtesy of Jeffrey L. Marshall, Heritage Conservancy 71; Kyle R. Weaver (courtesy of the Pennsylvania Historical and Museum Commission) 73, 74; Courtesy of Arcadia University 75; Courtesy of Berks County Heritage Center 76; Gerald M. Kuncio (courtesy of Pennsylvania Department of Transportation) 78, 79; Wikimedia Commons/By Smallbones - Own Work, CC0 81, 97, 123; Wikimedia Commons/By Difference Engine - Own Work, CC BY-SA 4.0 86; Courtesy of the Historic Preservation Trust of Berks County 89 (top and bottom); Flicker.com/By Jim, the Photographer - CC BY-SA 2.0 95; Courtesy of the Fairmount Park Conservancy 101; Peter Woodall 104; Courtesy of Pearl Buck International 107, 108; David Graham, Exhibition Hall (courtesy of Wagner Free Institute of Science) 132; Tom Crane, Lecture Hall (courtesy of Wagner Free Institute of Science) 133; Wikimedia Commons/By Susan Spitz - Own Work, CC BY-SA 4.0 134; Courtesy of Montgomery County Planning Commission 139; Courtesy of Wyck Association 141; Brian Butko 142, 161, 162; Tupungato/Getty Images 143; Wikimedia Commons/By Dllu - Own Work, CC BY-SA 4.0 144; Wikimedia Commons/By English Wikipedia user Daniel Case, CC BY-SA 3.0 145; Wikimedia Commons/By Jdh123149 at English Wikipedia, CC BY-SA 3.0 147; Historic American Engineering Record, Creator, and Cambria Iron Company. Cambria Iron Company, Blast Furnaces No. 5 & 6, Lower Works, Johnstown, Cambria County, PA. Cambria County Johnstown Pennsylvania, 1968. Documentation Compiled After. Photograph. https://www.loc .gov/item/pa3028/ 148; Wikimedia Commons/By Midnightdreary - Own Work, CC BY-SA 3.0 151, 152, 156; Mark N. Platts 159, 160; Ed Massery (courtesy of Meadowcroft Rockshelter and Historic Village) 163; Courtesy of Meadowcroft Rockshelter and Historic Village 164; Anthony Douglas Watson 165; Sarah Buffington (courtesy of the Pennsylvania Historical and Museum Commission) 166; Courtesy of the National Road Heritage Corridor 168; Wikimedia Commons/By Coasterlover1994 - Own Work, CC BY-SA 4.0 172; Historic American Engineering Record, Creator, William A Young, Carl Young, Walter Young, Robert Eicher, Andy Moore, Earl Crockard, et al., Lowe, Jet, photographer. W. A. Young & Sons Foundry & Machine Shop, On Water Street along Monongahela River, Rices Landing, Greene County, PA. Greene County Pennsylvania Rices Landing, 1968. Documentation Compiled After. Photograph. https://www.loc.gov/item/pa2222/ 174.

Acknowledgments

I would like to thank my incredible support system, who offered so much encouragement, access to photos, offers to read and proofread, and a few well-placed "You got this" e-mails and texts when I needed it most. Thank you to my editor, Sarah Parke, who patiently answered every question and continually offered encouragement throughout this process, and to Lynn Zelem, production editor, who helped a first-time author navigate the world of book editing and always timed my deadlines so I could have an extra weekend. A million thanks to the Board of Directors and staff of Preservation Pennsylvania who gave me time, assistance, and coffee whenever I needed it; to my colleagues in history and historic preservation who offered insight and their beautiful photographs for the book, especially Bonnie Halda, my fairy godmother of photography; to Cindy Gulden, my highly paid assistant (if you can count many thanks as a salary); and to those who said yes whenever I asked for something. I had many cheerleaders who provided the perfect type of cheer at the right time: Brian Butko, Julia Chain, Nathaniel Guest, Sabra Smith, and Philip Zimmerman. This book would not have been possible without the support of many people including Karen Arnold, Jennifer Carlson, Emily Cooperman, Cara Curtis, Dan DiPrinzio, Sally Elk, Susan Glassman, Libbie Hawes, Cynthia Hershey, Donna Holdorf, Emanuel Kelly, Gerry Kuncio, Barbara Landis, Jeffrey Marshall, Timothy Pavlic II, Mark Platts, Lee Rainey, Daniel Roe, Kate Schaffner, Jane Sheffield, Lucy Strackhouse, Carolyn Wallace, Anthony Douglas Watson, Kyle Weaver, Cathy Wegener, and Peter Woodall. Last, but certainly not least, thank you to my best friend and husband, Rodney Crawford, who lived through it all, read every entry, did a lot of dishes, picked up a lot of takeout, and just generally encouraged me through the whole process.

About the Author

A part-time job typing National Register Nominations in 1982 turned into a long career for Mindy Gulden Crawford. She has been the executive director of Preservation Pennsylvania since 2006, after spending 24 years at Historic York, Inc. (20 years as executive director). A bachelor's degree in business administration from York College coupled with a master's degree in historic preservation from Goucher College has opened many opportunities for work and volunteering. Mindy is an adjunct professor at Penn State Harrisburg and York College of Pennsylvania and serves on the Board of the National Alliance of Preservation Commissions.

In her spare time you'll find Mindy exploring the Lincoln Highway and other old roads searching for great roadside architecture and the perfect plastic snow globe. You might also find her wearing seven layers of period clothing to participate in Civil War dancing or living history events with her husband Rodney.